First-Rate Reading™ Basics

Comprehension
Grades 1–2

by Starin W. Lewis and
Elizabeth Suarez Aguerre

Carson-Dellosa Publishing Company, Inc. • Greensboro, North Carolina

Credits and Dedications

Project Director:
Kelly Gunzenhauser

Editors:
Ellen Gray White, Susan Traylor

Layout Design:
Jon Nawrocik

Inside Illustrations:
Stefano Giorgi

Cover Design:
Peggy Jackson

Cover Illustrations:
Stefano Giorgi

This book is dedicated to my friends and family. Thank you for encouraging me to follow my dreams. Your support has been overwhelming.

-S. L.

For my dearest friend, Beth, whom I love "more than that."

-E. S. A.

ISBN 1-59441-044-5

Table of Contents

Introduction 4
Parent Letter 5
Assessment 6
Pre-Reading Strategies 8
Monitoring Comprehension 15
Graphic and Semantic Organizers 23
Answering and Generating Comprehension Questions 34
Recognizing Story Structure 54
Summarizing 63
Interacting with Text 73

Introduction

Many reading teachers would argue that all reading instruction roads lead to comprehension. Understanding text is the ultimate goal of reading. Phonemic awareness, phonics, fluency, and vocabulary are all important to learn because they assist in comprehension. Without comprehension, reading is a futile pursuit. This book includes many activities to increase comprehension in first and second grades. Some of the activities are literature based, while others are general and can be used with various reading materials.

First-Rate Reading™ Basics: Comprehension assumes students have some knowledge of the other four skill sets and takes students beyond basic, word-for-word understanding that is often appropriate for the kindergarten level. Comprehension activities at this level assume that students can read and understand some text for themselves and are capable of searching for meaning through a variety of strategies. Comprehension instruction at this level also assumes that students are ready to make value judgments about the information they read, to determine whether they agree or disagree with it, and also to determine whether they like certain texts and make reading choices based on those likes or dislikes.

Utilize the reproducible Parent Letter (page 5) to help reinforce comprehension instruction at home. The more parents encourage reading and discussion, the more capable their children will be of understanding what they read. The Parent Letter helps inform parents about which skills they impart to their children while reading together and also offers suggestions for making reading experiences even more valuable to young readers.

Finally, use the Assessment (pages 6-7) to look at students' comprehension levels at any time during the school year, including before instruction begins. Giving assessment early will help you determine in which areas students need practice. It will also help you group students by skill level, even if your preference is to group students with a range of skills.

Name ______________________________

Parent Letter

Dear Parents/Family:

Research shows that good readers are more successful in school. Reading is used in all other subjects and is critical for success in real life. It is important for your child to develop a solid reading base that extends beyond phonics into other areas, such as comprehension. Following are suggestions and information about this area of instruction.

Comprehension is the purpose for reading. It allows the reader to make connections between the text and other texts or experiences. Help your child improve comprehension by doing the following:

- Be a good reading role model. Be sure your child sees you reading often.
- Make reading a reward. Use books and reading time as a reward for good behavior, school improvement, etc.
- Take your child to the library to check out books regularly and to attend programs, such as story time, puppet shows, etc.
- Help your child build a home library. An amazing feeling comes with owning books. Create a special bookshelf and let your child earn book money by doing chores or saving allowance.
- Have a weekly or nightly "Family Reading Time." Turn off televisions, computers, and phones, and read. Read a book together, or read independently and share what you are reading about.
- Discuss what your child is reading. Ask "thinking questions," such as, "What do you think will happen next? Why do you think the character did that? How would you feel if you were the character? If you could change anything about the story, what would it be? What's happened so far?"
- Read sections of the newspaper together. Discuss the articles.
- Purchase or borrow books on tape. Have your child listen to a story and follow along with the text.
- Ask your child questions, such as, "What do you like most/least about this story? What do you think will happen next? What is this story about? What happened at the beginning/middle/end?"

Using these ideas will help your child improve reading comprehension. For more information, please feel free to contact me.

Sincerely,

____

Directions for Comprehension Assessment

Use the following questions for individual assessment. Copy the Comprehension Assessment reproducible (page 7) to record individual student's responses. Modify the language as needed for younger students who may need to dictate their responses. For older or more advanced students, read the questions aloud to small groups and let students record their own answers.

1. **Skills: Monitoring comprehension and strategies for self-correction**
   Say, "Pretend that you are reading and come to a word that you do not know. Tell three things you could do to help you figure out the meaning of the word." (Have advanced students write the strategies.)

2. **Skill: Using graphic organizers (This example uses a Venn diagram. If desired, assess students with a different graphic organizer.)**
   Say, "Think about one of your friends. How are you and your friend alike? How are you different? Show me where to write the similarities and differences in the diagram." (Have students complete diagrams on separate sheets of paper.)

For the remaining questions, choose a book that is new to students and follow the steps to complete the assessment.

3. **Skill: Pre-reading strategies**
   Show the cover and ask, "What do you think this story will be about? Tell me your prediction." (Have advanced students write predictions.)

4. **Skills: Generating comprehension questions and pre-reading strategies**
   Say, "What is a question that you think the book will answer?" (Have advanced students write questions.)

5. **Skills: Recognizing story structure and answering explicit comprehension questions**
   Read the new book aloud. Ask, "Who are the main characters of the story? Write them next to number 5."

6. **Skills: Recognizing story structure and answering explicit comprehension questions.**
   Ask, "What is the book's setting?" or "Where did the story take place?" Have students write their answers.

7. **Skill: Answering implicit comprehension questions**
   Choose a part of the book where a character shows emotion, but the emotion is not directly stated. Show the page and ask, "What do you think the character is feeling here? Why?" Have students write their answers.

8. **Skill: Answering scripted comprehension questions**
   Using the same emotion as in question number seven, say, "Write a few sentences about a time that you felt the same way." (Have younger students draw pictures of the events and dictate the circumstances.)

9. **Skill: Summarizing**
   Say, "On a separate sheet of paper, write a short summary of the story." (Have younger students draw and label pictures.)

10. **Skill: Responding to text**
    Ask, "What was your favorite part of the story and why?" (Have students respond orally, if possible.)

Name ______________________________

Date ______________________________

Comprehension Assessment

Follow the directions your teacher gives you to complete the page.

1. a. ______________________________
   b. ______________________________
   c. ______________________________

2. On a separate sheet of paper, follow your teacher's directions to fill in a diagram.

3. ______________________________

4. ______________________________

5. ______________________________

6. ______________________________

7. ______________________________

8. ______________________________

9. On a separate sheet of paper, write a short summary of the story.

10. Answer the question your teacher asks.

Pre-Reading Strategies

Introduction

Most people recognize the importance of post-reading comprehension activities, but teaching pre-reading strategies is vital, as well. Improve students' skills by teaching pre-reading comprehension strategies, such as previewing the text, looking at text features, building on prior knowledge, making predictions, reviewing vocabulary, and setting a purpose for reading. These skills will help students' reading comprehension at all stages of reading.

Preview with Think-Alouds

Students need to be taught to preview before reading new material. Explain that previewing (looking at the title, front cover, back cover, chapter titles, headings, subheadings, and photos) is like a warm-up for the brain. Previewing helps the brain "get ready" for the information it will receive. Guide students through this process by thinking aloud as you preview. For example, say, "Before I start reading this book, I look at the title and the cover's illustrations to get an idea of what it might be about. The title is *Thank You, Mr. Falker* by Patricia Polacco (Philomel, 1998), and I see an illustration of a girl sitting at a desk and a man standing next to her. Maybe he is her teacher. I can tell by the look on her face that she is upset. I wonder if the man is Mr. Falker and if the girl is going to thank him for helping her in school." Proceed to read the book aloud for students, pausing to make connections between the previewed material and the reading as needed. When reading articles or textbooks, follow a similar format to teach students to preview the titles, headings, subheadings, bold type, photographs, captions, etc.

Preview with a Twist

This nonfiction preview can be used with any nonfiction text. As an example, select a nonfiction book about tornadoes, such as *Do Tornadoes Really Twist?: Questions and Answers About Tornadoes and Hurricanes* by Melvin and Gilda Berger (Scholastic, 2000). Review the features of nonfiction books (tables of contents, indexes, chapter headings, charts, tables, graphs, captions, maps, etc.). Preview the book with students to see which features it contains. Fill in any features that are not listed on the Twisting Tornado Features reproducible (page 9) and give each student a copy. Guide students through the checklist and ask, "Does this nonfiction book have a table of contents?" Look through the book with students to find the first element. As you read the book aloud, instruct students to look for each feature and to check off each element that they see in the book. After completing the checklist, have each student cut out the spiral and then cut along the dashed line until she reaches the center. When students hold up the bigger ends, the spirals should look like twisting tornadoes. Hang the twisting tornadoes from a clothesline suspended near the classroom ceiling.

Twisting Tornado Features

Look for each feature in the book.
If you find it, draw a check in its box. If you do not, leave the box blank. Cut out the shape and then cut on the dashed lines.

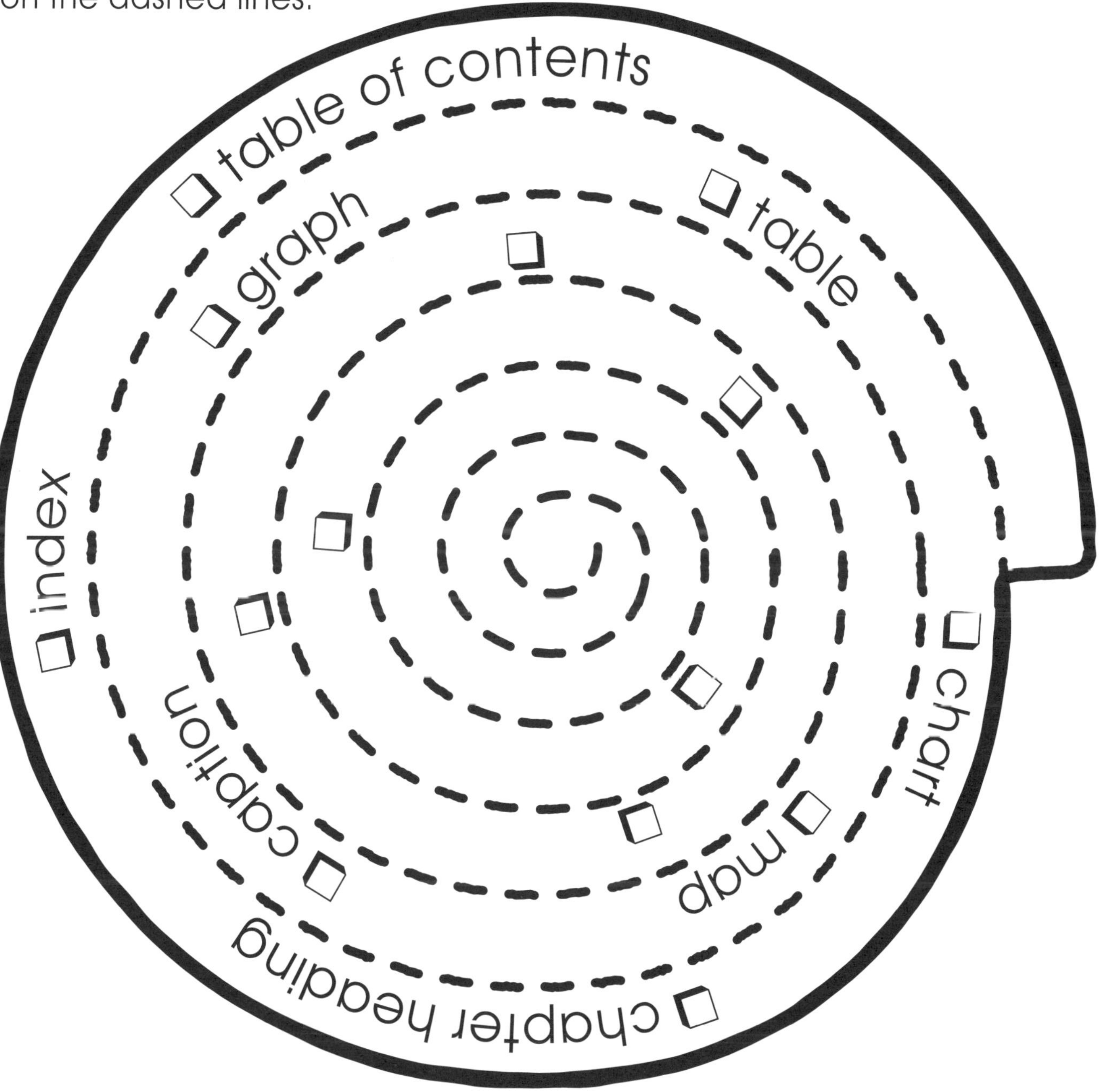

A Desert Animal

Use predictions to set a purpose for reading. Use *How Jackrabbit Got His Very Long Ears* by Heather Irbinskas (Rising Moon, 1994) to demonstrate how students can make predictions about stories they read. Ask, "What is a jackrabbit? What does it look like?" (A jackrabbit is a desert rabbit with very long ears.) Give each student a large piece of brown construction paper. Have her draw a large circle near the bottom of the paper for a rabbit face. Then, have her draw two very long rabbit ears on top of the circle that extend to the top of the paper. Have each student cut out the rabbit head and ears. Explain that this book is a fable, not a true story. Ask, "How do you think jackrabbits got their very long ears?" Tell students to be creative in their explanations. Have students write their responses on the ears of their jackrabbits, then let students decorate the faces. Read the book aloud, then have students compare their stories to the book. Display the jackrabbits at a reading center along with a copy of the book cover. Let students read each other's predictions before rereading the book independently.

Word Guess

This vocabulary activity is particularly effective with informational text, which students also benefit from previewing. As with fiction, have students preview text by looking at the titles, headings, subheadings, photographs, etc. Instruct students to list vocabulary words they think they will encounter while reading. Model this so that students get an idea of the thought process involved. For example, preview an article about storms prior to reading it aloud. Create a list of vocabulary words by thinking aloud, "I think one of the words in this article might be *hurricane*, so I'm going to write that on my list. I think I will see this word because the article will be about storms, and I noticed that one of the headings is Types of Storms. A hurricane is one type of storm." If students are proficient at writing, have each student create a study guide by listing the words in a column on a sheet of paper, then writing definitions next to the words as they are defined in the text.

The Magic of Predictions

Demonstrate another way students can set a purpose for reading. Compare previewing and making good story predictions that lead to understanding a book to pulling a rabbit out of a hat. The "magic" in setting a purpose happens when a student "pulls an idea out of the hat" that helps her search for clues to understanding a story. Preview a current book's cover and inside illustrations. Have students make predictions about the plot while looking at the illustrations. Slowly turn the pages so that the class sees each illustration. Explain that sometimes rabbits and other items come out of magicians' special top hats. Provide students with enlarged copies of the Abracadabra reproducible (page 12). Have each student write the book's title and a story prediction on the top hat pattern. Then, read the story aloud. Direct students to write or draw what really happened on the rabbit pattern and cut out the hat and rabbit. Help each student cut a slit on the dashed line on the hat, then pull the smaller end of the rabbit through the slit in the top hat from the back of the hat. Each student should be able to pull her rabbit (what really happened) out of her hat. Have students take turns sharing their initial predictions on the top hats, then pulling out the rabbits to show what they wrote or drew about the story's real plot.

Writing to Compare

Select a fiction book with an interesting cover illustration. Stimulate interest in the book by hiding the title while showing the cover, then ask, "What do you think happens in the book?" Have each student write or dictate a short story that could be in the book. Let students share stories with classmates. Read the book aloud and have students compare their stories to the real one. Were they close? What was the story really about? Finally, discuss with students how writing their own stories and comparing them helped them understand the book.

Connecting with Prior Knowledge

Activating students' prior knowledge helps them connect with a topic. This activity can be used with any topic. For example, if students will be studying lighthouses and are unfamiliar with them, read a nonfiction book or article about lighthouses. Give each student an enlarged copy of the Lighthouse Knowledge reproducible (page 13). Direct students to write the title of the book on the line provided, then write everything they know about lighthouses on the lighthouse pattern. Ask, "What is a lighthouse? What does it do? Where do you usually find lighthouses? What do they look like?" After students finish writing about lighthouses, introduce *The Little Red Lighthouse and the Great Gray Bridge* by Hildegarde H. Swift (Harcourt & Brace, 2003) or another fiction book about lighthouses. This story is about a lighthouse and a bridge in New York City. While the story is fiction, the bridge and lighthouse are real. Show students where New York City and the Hudson River are on a map. Read the book aloud. Have students color and cut out their lighthouses. Display the lighthouses on a bulletin board titled "Seeing the Light of Comprehension."

Abracadabra

Write the book title and a story prediction on the hat. Write or draw what actually happened on the rabbit. Cut on the dashed lines. Slide the rabbit through the slit to pull the rabbit out of the hat.

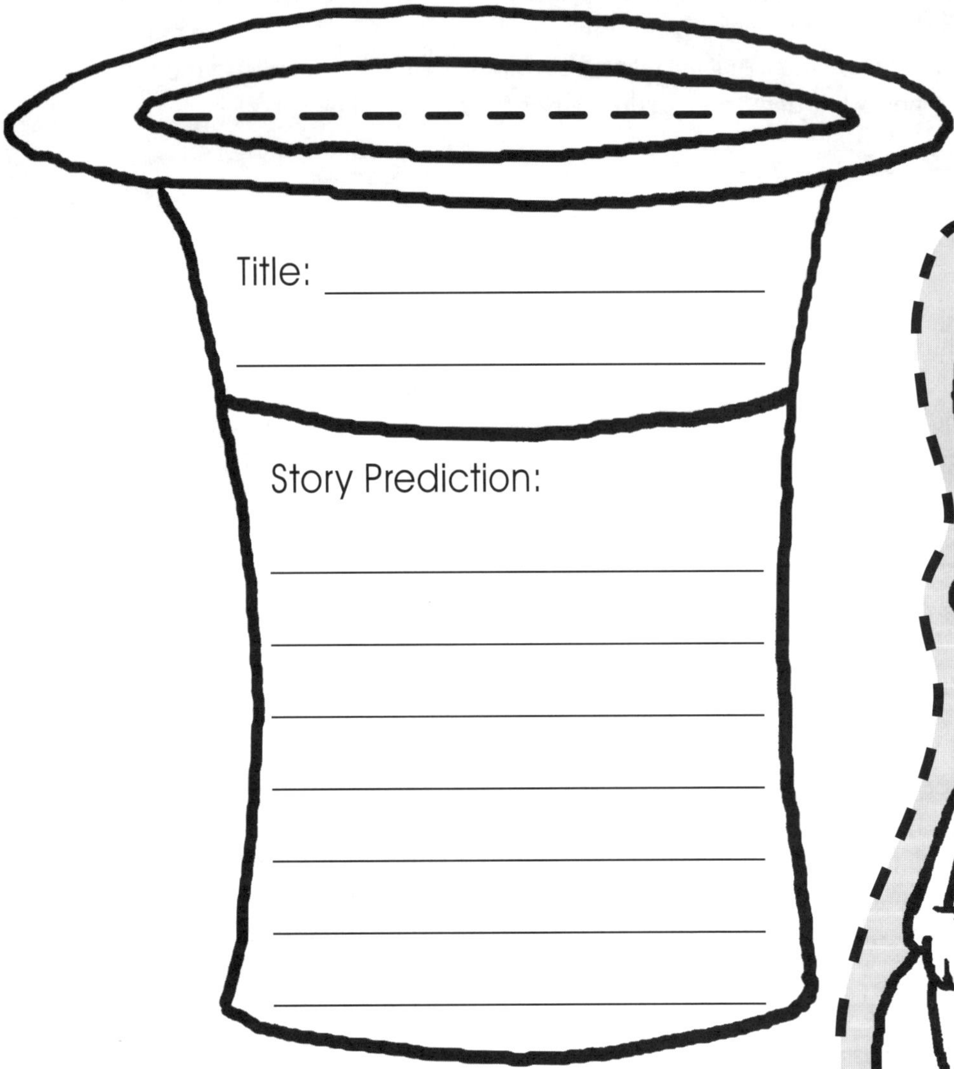

Name ______________________________

Lighthouse Knowledge

Write everything you know about lighthouses in the pattern below.

Character Sketch

Have students focus on the lead character to help them understand a fiction story. As an example, select a fiction book that is centered around an animal and gives a clue about the animal's appearance in the title. Introduce the book by telling students the type of animal, its name, and the title of the book. Three possible examples are *Henry and Mudge and the Happy Cat* by Cynthia Rylant (Simon & Schuster, 1994), *Harry the Dirty Dog* by Gene Zion (HarperCollins, 1976), and *The Rainbow Fish* by Marcus Pfister (North-South Books, 1992). Give each student a piece of paper and crayons to draw a picture of the main character before he sees a picture of him. Have students think about the title of the book before completing their drawings. Then, reveal the cover of the book. Have students compare their pictures of the animal to the illustrator's picture. Read the story aloud. Explain that by drawing the main character ahead of time, students focused more on the main character when they listened to the book being read. Repeat with other books using main characters or minor characters.

Stop, Look, Listen

Students may become so intent on finishing an assignment that they forget to pause to monitor comprehension during reading. As students become more fluent, they may get to the end of a passage or book and find themselves asking, "What did I just read?" Help students avoid this behavior by initiating a "stop, look, listen" reading session. Choose a day where all students have the same reading assignment to complete. Allow students to begin reading. After several minutes, say, "Stop, look, listen!" At this time, students should stop reading, look back through the book to remind themselves of what happened, and talk with classmates about what has happened so far. Over time, students will develop a habit of stopping and thinking about the book as they are reading it.

Define the Purpose

To focus students' attention on the story and increase comprehension, help them set a purpose for reading. Use a book with illustrations that will intrigue students. Introduce the story and show the book cover and several illustrations. Encourage students to ask questions. Write students' questions on the board. Then, say, "Our purpose for reading today is to see if your questions are answered in the story." Review the student-generated questions, then read the book. As students hear answers to their questions, have them raise their hands. Discuss any unanswered questions on the chart paper and ask if the book had the answers (it may not). Tell students that asking questions before reading a book can help them focus on the story better.

Monitoring Comprehension

Introduction

Monitoring is a vital comprehension strategy. Good readers know when they understand text and when they do not. They can check themselves while reading and recognize when the text does not make sense. Teach students how to monitor themselves while reading, as well as what to do if they do not understand the text.

Identifying Story Elements with Flap Books

Flap books make excellent tools for identifying story elements or listing facts from informational text. Have each student fold a sheet of construction paper in half lengthwise. Have each student cut slits vertically in the top fold to form flaps. The number of slits should be one less than the number of elements you want students to cover. Then, have each student lift each flap and write inside. Students can also write on the outsides of the flaps and illustrate inside. Below are several effective ways to use flap books. Provide students with copies of the Flap Book reproducible (page 16) for directions for how to make a flap book.

- Use flap books with nonfiction that contains content students need to memorize. Have students create questions to write on the flaps and write the answers inside. Then, have students exchange flap books to study for tests, quiz each other, etc.
- Have each student identify and illustrate the beginning, middle, and end of a story.
- Have each student list and illustrate main story events.
- Have each student write the main idea on the outside of the large flap before cutting slits. Then, have her cut enough flaps to list a supporting detail under each flap.
- Have each student list a problem in the story, give possible solutions, and give the actual solution.

Retelling with Props

Students can monitor their comprehension by retelling a story in their own words. If they cannot retell the story, they may not understand what happened. Students will enjoy using props to retell. Select a book with a character that can be made into a puppet, such as *Henry and Mudge and the Bedtime Thumps* by Cynthia Rylant (Simon & Schuster, 1996). Let each student create a puppet of Mudge, the dog. Provide students with paper bags, construction paper scraps, and art supplies. Show pictures of Mudge to give students ideas and assist them with creating the puppets if necessary. (Explain that the fold of the bag is typically where the mouth goes.) Pair students after they finish their Mudge puppets. Read the first two chapters of the book. Direct students to use their Mudge puppets to retell the story to their partners; one partner should retell while the other listens and confirms whether "Mudge" was correct. Read the third chapter and have partners switch roles. Have students alternate roles with the remaining chapters. Consider grouping three students if one is ESL or is a less skilled conversationalist than his classmates. In a group of three, one student can help prompt the storyteller while the third listens.

Flap Book

Follow the directions to create a flap book. Your teacher will tell you what to draw or write on the book.

1. Fold a piece of paper in half.

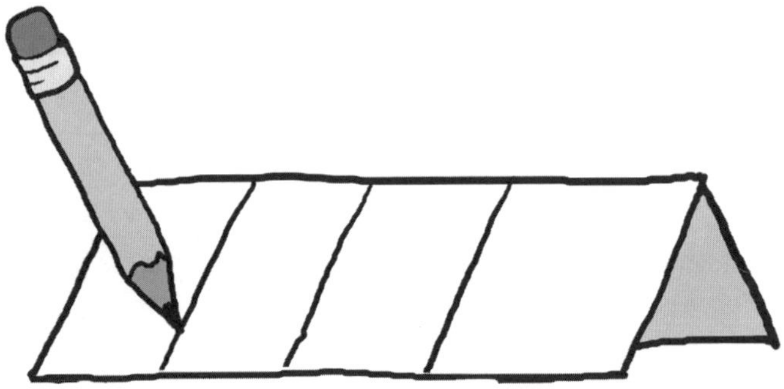

2. Draw three lines to make four sections on the front flap.

3. Cut the lines to the middle of the paper. Do not cut past the fold.

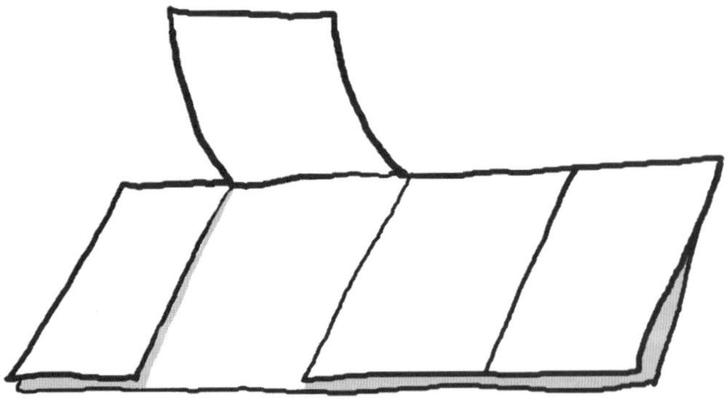

4. You can draw or write on top of the flaps or underneath.

Comprehension Toolbox

Explain that students need to actively try to understand what they are reading. There are several tools they can use when they do not understand text. Brainstorm different strategies students can use to help them understand text. Write their suggestions on the board. Be sure to include "fix-it" strategies, such as *go back and reread the sentence, use pictures to figure out meaning, use the context of the words, sound out a difficult word, look back in the story to find clues,* and *glance forward in the text.* Explain that these ideas are tools they can use if they need to "fix" comprehension problems. Give each student an enlarged copy of the Comprehension Toolbox reproducible (page 18). (Provide additional copies for students who want to write more than four strategies.) Direct students to cut out each tool and write a "fix-it" strategy on it. Have each student store his tools in a "toolbox" (envelope or folder). As students read, have them place their tools on their desks. Encourage students to use one or several of the reading tools when they do not understand part of a book.

Helpful Arrows

Create a visual reminder to help students understand and use the comprehension strategy of looking ahead and looking back in their reading. On construction paper, draw and cut out an arrow large enough for a student to write a short sentence on each side. On the arrow, write *Look back in the story* and color this side red. Turn over the arrow and write *Look forward in the story.* Color this side green. Explain that when a student realizes he does not understand something, a good strategy is to look back over the story to find the answer. If that does not work, sometimes it means the answer is coming up in the story. He can look ahead a little bit to see if the confusion will be cleared up soon. Show the front and back of your arrow. Tell students that this arrow will help them remember these two strategies. Read a book and stop at certain points in the story to model how to look back and forward. Use the paper arrow as a visual cue to help students remember this strategy. After the story, give students red and green construction paper to make their own arrows.

Name ______________________________

Comprehension Toolbox

Cut out each tool. Write a strategy on each tool. Use the tools to help you understand what you are reading.

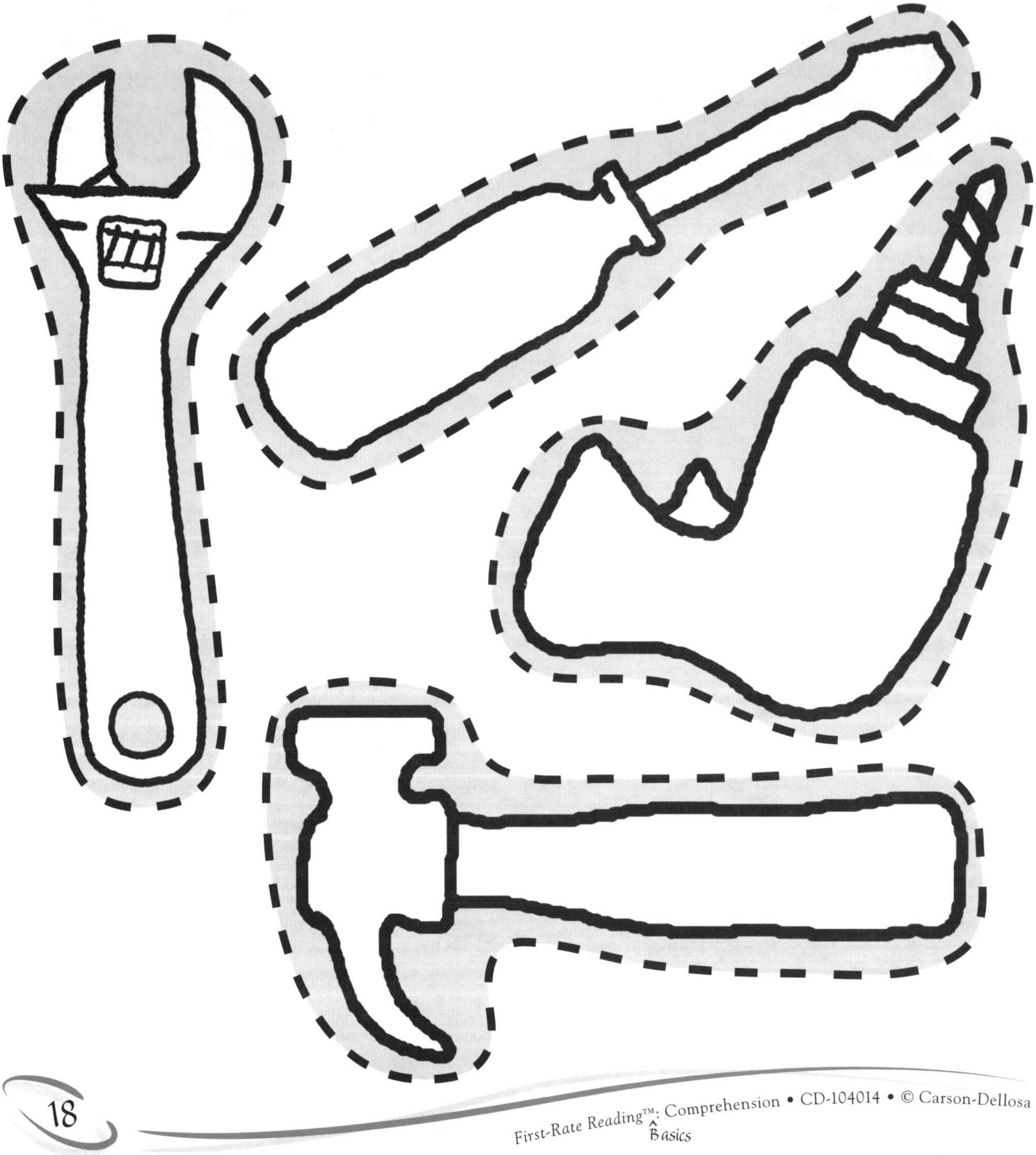

Reading Log

Review strategies that students can use to aid their comprehension while reading, then have them practice these strategies independently. Give each student a copy of the Reading Log (page 20). During independent reading time, have each student write the title of her book in the first column. When she comes to a place in the story that she does not understand, have her write the page number and sentence in the middle column, then pick a strategy from the menu that she thinks will work. Have her try more than one strategy if the first one does not work. Direct the student to write the strategy that works in the third column. Suggest that students try up to three strategies. If they still cannot understand what they are reading, suggest they continue reading. Do not allow a student to spend too much time on one passage. Have students use their reading logs each time they read independently in class. Periodically, have students compare which strategies worked for them for different stories.

It's a Mystery

Mysteries are a natural genre to pique students' interest in comprehension. Select a mystery to read aloud for this activity, such as a book from the *Nate the Great* series by Marjorie Weinman Sharmat (Yearling Books). Draw two columns on chart paper. Write *What we know* above one column and *What we do not know* above the other. Explain how important it is for students to be aware of what they know and do not know while they are reading. To practice, have students try to solve the mystery in the story. Read the book and stop at certain points in the story to have students identify what they know and what they do not know. By making these identifications, students' investigative skills become vital comprehension skills.

Sticky Notes

Sticky notes can act as more than just "flags." They can supply helpful cues about what readers want to discuss after reading. Teach students to use sticky notes while reading to help them monitor their comprehension, read actively, and initiate post-reading discussions. Before having students do this independently, model the process by using think-aloud techniques on an overhead projector or chart paper. Give each student a pad of sticky notes. As the student reads, instruct her to write questions, comments, thoughts, etc., on the sticky notes and stick each note on the corresponding page. Make sure students write the page numbers on the notes in case any fall off. These sticky notes can be used afterward to initiate discussions in small groups, pairs, or as a whole class. Have students return to the beginning of the material and refer to their notes to begin the discussion.

Reading Log

Write the book's title in the first column.
Write parts you do not understand in the second column.
Write down strategies you used in the third column.

Reading Strategy Menu

- Reread the text.
- Try to sound out a difficult word.
- Look at the pictures for clues.
- Look back in the story to see if you missed something.
- Glance ahead to see if your question is answered later.

Book Title	I do not understand...	Strategy Used

Illustration Interpretations

Explain that good readers check to make sure they understand what they are reading. Teach students to use illustrations prior to and during reading to decode meaning from the text. Use a book with funny illustrations to demonstrate, such as *Diary of a Worm* by Doreen Cronin (HarperCollins, 2003). Give each student a piece of brown paper. Direct students to accordion fold their papers five times. (The paper should be long enough so that students are able to write a few sentences on each folded section, so adjust the size of the paper according to the average size of students' handwriting.) Have each student draw a worm face in the first section of the paper and add the title *Diary of a Worm*. Show students the first illustrated diary page and have each student write what he thinks is happening on the first section of his worm. Then, read the text for that page aloud to allow students to see if their ideas from the illustrations were accurate. Mention that it is fine if their answers are not the same as the text because people can interpret illustrations differently. Let students continue to write what they think the illustrations depict throughout the rest the book until they fill up all sections of their worms. Ask students if they felt the pictures helped them understand the story and discuss which picture clues added new meaning to the text sentences. Allow students to share their versions of what they thought the illustrations were showing. Then, read the entire story from beginning to end. Have students draw and cut out red construction paper baseball hats to glue to the heads of their worms. Create a bulletin board titled "We Are Bookworms" by attaching the paper worms so that the folds stick out from the bulletin board.

"Monitor"-ing Comprehension

When students have trouble understanding a story, give them some "key" ideas to solve the problem. Give each student a copy of the "Monitor"-ing Comprehension reproducible (page 22). Explain that the computer monitor will help students remember to monitor their comprehension. Have students read the following sentences on the monitor section of the reproducible: *While reading, monitor what you do understand. Stop when you do not understand something.* Have students read the following "key" concepts on the keyboard section of the reproducible to help them understand what they are reading.

- Go back and reread the sentence.
- Use the pictures.
- Use the meaning (context) of the words.
- Sound out a hard word.
- Look back in the story to find clues.
- Glance ahead to see if future pages will answer questions.

Have each student cut out his computer and fold it on the line between the monitor and keyboard so that the reproducible looks like a computer monitor with a keyboard in front of it. Allow students to keep their computers at their desks for reference or create a bulletin board of student computers titled "Monitor-ing Our Comprehension."

"Monitor"-ing Comprehension

Read the "key" ways you can fix your comprehension if you are having problems. Cut out the picture and fold on the line between the computer and keyboard.

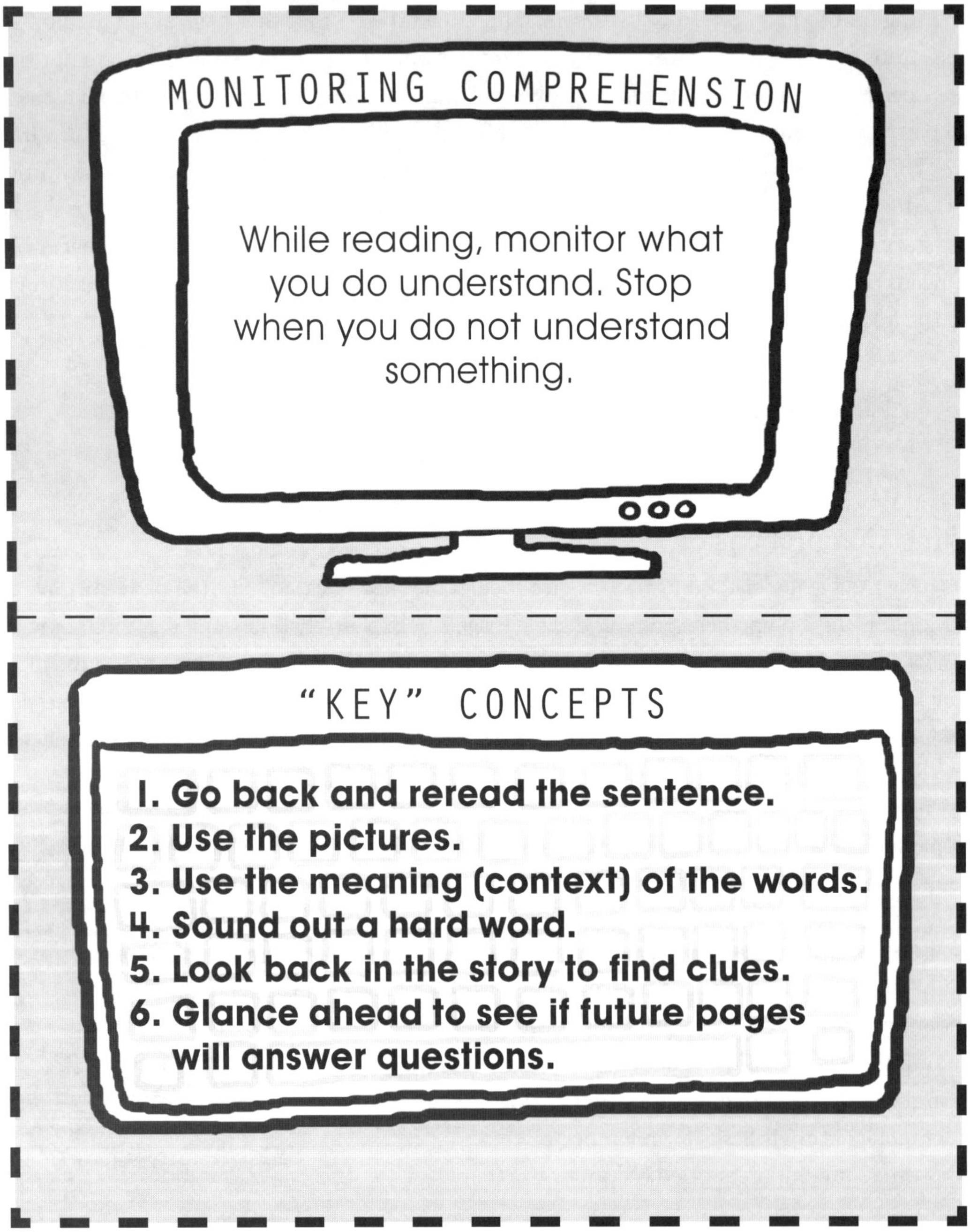

Graphic and Semantic Organizers

Introduction

Graphic and semantic organizers are visual tools students can use to organize information from texts. These organizers can include diagrams, charts, graphs, webs, maps, etc. Students may use graphic organizers with fiction or nonfiction. The pictorial aspect of a graphic organizer allows students to see connections between text elements.

What's the Same? What's Different?

Use the books *If You Give a Pig a Pancake* (HarperCollins, 1998) and *If You Give a Mouse a Cookie* by Laura Joffe Numeroff (HarperCollins, 1985). Prepare circle patterns approximately 4" (10 cm) in diameter for students to trace. Give each student a piece of light brown construction paper. Direct each student to use the patterns to trace two circles that overlap in the middle to create a Venn diagram. Have students draw chocolate chips in the first circle and lightly color the second circle to look like a pancake. Have students write *If You Give a Mouse a Cookie* near the first circle and *If You Give a Pig a Pancake* near the second circle. Have students write *Both* in the overlap. Draw a Venn diagram on the board as a model. First read one book, then the other. As you read the second book, have students think about what is the same and what is different about the two books. For young students, pause periodically and fill in the diagram on the board following students' suggestions. For more advanced students, after reading the books, have students compare and contrast the two stories. Have students write things that are different in the two separate circles. Have them write things that are the same in the middle section. When students finish, direct them to cut around the two circles, leaving the overlap intact. Staple the students' circles to a bulletin board. Add the title "What's the Same? What's Different?" To celebrate the activity, consider offering chocolate chip cookies to students or be extra creative and offer chocolate chip pancakes, prepared before class, to celebrate the overlap. Before completing any food activity, ask parental permission and inquire about students' food allergies and religious or other preferences.

Stacks of Story Mapping

Have students use this graphic organizer to focus on the beginning, middle, and end of a story. Typically, the beginning introduces the characters and setting, the middle has a problem and a resolution, and the end usually clears up any unanswered questions. The beginning, middle, and end are all part of the plot. Demonstrate this concept as you read *Too Many Tamales* by Gary Soto (Putnam, 1996). First, help students identify the beginning, middle, and end of the story. Then, give each student an enlarged copy of the A Stack of Tamales reproducible (page 24). Explain that there are three tamales on the page. In the top tamale, have students write the beginning of the story. Have students write the problem and its resolution in the middle tamale. Challenge students to think of how the story wrapped up any loose ends and summarize this in the bottom tamale. Have each student compare answers with a classmate.

Name ______________________________

A Stack of Tamales

Write the beginning, middle, and end of the book *Too Many Tamales* in the correct tamales.

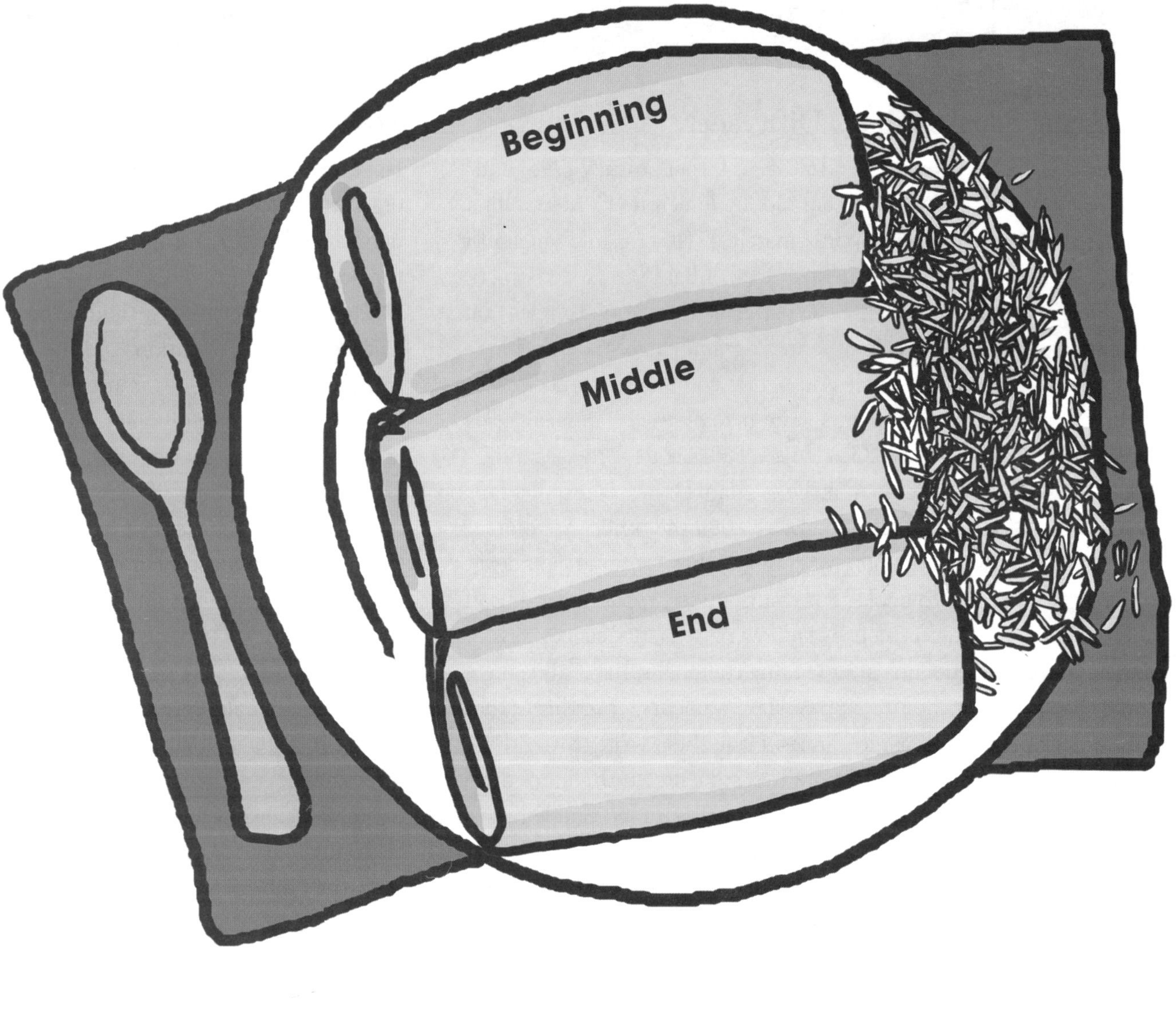

Character Study

Creating a visual organizer to help students analyze a main character helps students understand how that character helps drive the story. Select a book that has an animal as the main character, such as *Wemberly Worried* by Kevin Henkes (Greenwillow Books, 2000) or *Livingstone Mouse* by Pamela Duncan Edwards (HarperCollins, 1998). Show students the book cover and ask questions that relate to clues given in the illustration or title, such as, "Who do you think is the main character? How does she feel? How can you tell?" Students should respond with information from the title. For example, for the book *Wemberly Worried,* students might respond, "The mouse on the cover looks worried." As you read, have students think of words (or traits) that describe the mouse's personality rather than her physical appearance. After reading the book, have students suggest words that describe the main character (*worried, nervous, friendly, happy, musical, playful,* etc.). Give each student a piece of white construction paper. Provide crayons and markers. Have each student draw an ice cream cone shape. Have her add two mouse ears, a nose, two eyes, and eyebrows. Instruct them to color the mouse. Then, have each student draw six whiskers, three on each side of the nose. Direct students to write six words that describe the character on the whiskers. Display the mouse pictures on a bulletin board titled "(Mouse's name) Is a Character!"

Character Development

Use the book *Verdi* by Janell Cannon (Harcourt, 1996) to show students how to evaluate character development. Give each student one green and one yellow piece of construction paper. Instruct students to put one piece on top of the other. Staple the corners and have each student draw a snake on the yellow side and cut it out while keeping the two pieces of paper together. Direct students to glue the snakes together and add faces with crayons or markers. Before reading, ask students to think of words to describe the python Verdi when he is yellow and young and also when he is green and older. As you read, pause to have each student write at least five words that describe Verdi when he was young, such as *impatient, fidgety, reckless,* etc., on the yellow side of his snake. On the green side, have each student write at least five words that describe Verdi when he was older, such as *fun, slower, cautious,* etc. Young students may need to dictate words. Punch a hole in the head and tail of each paper snake, attach thread or fishing line across the classroom, and hang each snake from it to resemble Verdi flying through the air. Or, create a bulletin board by letting students finger paint a jungle background and add the snakes to it.

Alike but Different

Relating personal experiences to those of a main character can help students have a deeper understanding of the story. *Chrysanthemum* by Kevin Henkes (HarperCollins, 1991) is about a mouse by the same name. Read the book aloud and give each student a copy of the Alike but Different reproducible (page 27). While you read the book, have each student think about how he is alike or different from Chrysanthemum, especially when thinking about the character's experiences at school. Work with students to compare and contrast Chrysanthemum and themselves using the diagrams. Have students write or draw descriptions of themselves in the circles labeled *you*. Have students record descriptions about Chrysanthemum in the circle with her name. Then, let students list similarities in the overlapping space between the circles. Use additional copies of the reproducible to compare characters, books, etc.

Inside the Emotion

Strong emotions in stories are the ones that are easiest for young students to connect with. Read a book that includes a character who gets angry and reacts strongly to her situation. Good choices are *When Sophie Gets Angry—Really, Really Angry . . .* by Molly Bang (Scholastic, 1999) and *Don't Let the Pigeon Drive the Bus* by Mo Willems (Hyperion Books, 2003). Read the book and ask students, "What made the main character angry?" Record responses on the board. Continue to ask questions, such as, "What did the character do when she was angry? Did this make her more or less angry? Did it solve the problem? How did the character finally solve the problem?" Continue to record answers on the board. Then, give each student two pieces of paper and crayons or markers. Ask each student to draw an angry face on one piece of paper and a happy face on another piece of paper. Next to the faces, let students write and draw things from the story that made the character angry and happy. Then, ask them to circle things on the happy papers that helped solve the problem. If desired, repeat this activity but let individual students write things about themselves that made them angry and things that solved the problems.

Name ________________________________

Alike but Different

In the circles, draw or write things that describe you and Chrysanthemum. In the part that overlaps, draw or write things you have in common.

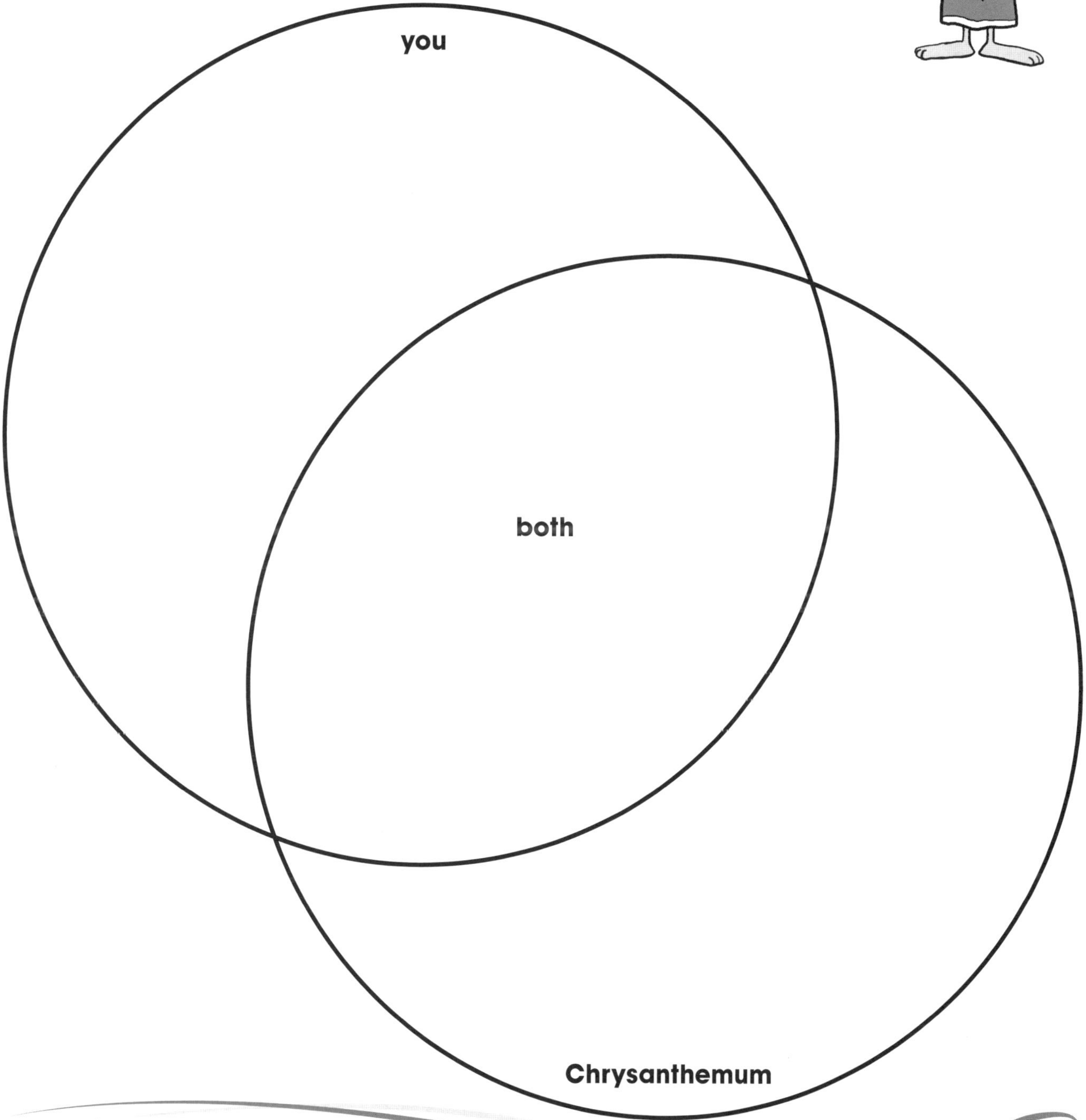

A Pad of Summaries

Explain that sometimes pictures can help readers focus on a story and understand it better. As an example, use pictures to summarize the chapter book *Frog and Toad Are Friends* by Arnold Lobel (HarperCollins, 1979). Give each student a piece of blue construction paper and a piece of green construction paper. Provide large, plastic cups for students to use as patterns for drawing lily pad circles. Direct each student to trace six circles on green construction paper and cut them out. Then, have each student draw and cut out a triangle from the center of each circle to the outside of the circle to make a lily pad. Have each student write the chapter titles and numbers on his first five lily pads. The titles are *1. Spring, 2. The Story, 3. A Lost Button, 4. A Swim,* and *5. The Letter.* On the sixth lily pad, have him write *Frog and Toad Are Friends.* Read the book, but stop reading after the first chapter and have each student write or draw a summary of it on the lily pad titled *1. Spring.* Repeat the same steps with each chapter, then review the chapters in order. Finally, have each student summarize the entire book on the lily pad titled *Frog and Toad Are Friends.* Encourage students not to repeat the exact words from their chapter summaries but to combine all five into a summary of the book. Have each student glue his lily pads onto the blue paper with the *Frog and Toad Are Friends* lily pad in the center and the other lily pads in sequential order around the center.

Main Idea Construction

Stating the main idea is the same as telling what the story is about. Help students focus on the story and make connections using graphic organizers. When students figure out the main idea, they will also find that there are details in the story that support the main idea. As an example, read *Horace and Morris but Mostly Dolores* by James Howe (Simon & Schuster, 1999). While you read, encourage students to think about the main idea. Discuss the story events and help students identify the main idea of the story. (Students may identify it as something similar to "You shouldn't discriminate" or "You should include your friends in clubs.") Write the main idea on the board, then ask, "What are some details that support this main idea?" Have students suggest supporting details and write at least four of these on the board. Then, give each student a copy of the Main Idea Construction reproducible (page 29). Have each student write the main idea on the clubhouse roof. Direct each student to write supporting details on the side of the clubhouse. Use the Main Idea Construction reproducible to give students additional practice in identifying the main idea and supporting details of other books.

Name ______________________________

Main Idea Construction

Write the main idea on the lines on the clubhouse roof. Write details on the lines on the side of the clubhouse.

Cloud Types

Graphic organizers can be as useful with nonfiction text as they are with fiction. For example, use a graphic organizer at a science center. Place several books about clouds, blue construction paper, cotton balls, and glue at the center. Post the Cloud Types Directions reproducible (page 31) at the center. Familiarize students with vocabulary by reviewing the basic cloud types (cumulus, cirrus, and stratus) before letting them visit the center. For lower-level readers, post a reference page showing and describing the different cloud types. Give each student a copy of the Cloud Types reproducible (page 32) to complete. Display the reproducibles on a bulletin board covered with cotton batting.

Curriculum Webbing

Place several nonfiction books about spiders at a center. Provide white paper plates and markers or crayons. Explain that a word web has a topic in the middle. Write the word *spiders* on the board and draw a circle around it. Draw lines that extend from the center to make it look like a spiderweb. Write categories and vocabulary related to spiders, like *habitats, food, webs, eight legs,* etc., on the web. Have students make word webs about specific spiders. Direct each student to choose a spider from one of the books at the center and draw it in the middle of the back of a paper plate. Have each student write the name of his spider in the center of the picture and draw lines from the spider to the outside of the plate. Then, have each student write interesting facts, such as *food, habitat, venom*, etc., on the lines. Use yarn to dangle the finished plates from a bulletin board titled "Spiderwebs."

Literature Comparisons

Check out a classic version of *The Three Little Pigs* and a different version, such as *The Three Pigs* by David Wiesner (Houghton Mifflin, 2001). Explain that very old stories called *fairy tales* have been around so long that sometimes there are different versions, such as the classic and updated versions of *The Three Little Pigs*. Read aloud the two books. Ask students to think about the differences and similarities in the two stories. Ask, "What was the same in the two stories?" Students may identify the pigs; the wolf; houses of straw, sticks, bricks; etc. Ask, "What was different in the two stories?" Students may note that in one book, the three pigs leave the story and have a different adventure. Give each student a copy of the Comparing the Three Little Pigs reproducible (page 33). Tell students that using this graphic organizer will help them organize their thoughts. Have each student write the similarities in the house that has *Both Stories* written on the roof. Direct each student to write the differences in the houses marked *Classic Story* and *New Story*.

Name ______________________________

Cloud Types Directions

Read some of the books about cloud types and look at the pictures.

On the Cloud Types page, write a few words that describe each main type of cloud: cumulus, cirrus, and stratus.

Then, use cotton balls to make each type of cloud. Glue the clouds to a piece of blue paper.

Cloud Types

Look at the names
of the three main types of clouds below.
Follow the directions posted in the center.

Cumulus	Cirrus	Stratus
______	______	______
______	______	______
______	______	______
______	______	______
______	______	______
______	______	______
______	______	______
______	______	______
______	______	______
______	______	______
______	______	______
______	______	______

Name ________________________________

Comparing the Three Little Pigs

Read or listen to two versions of *The Three Little Pigs*. Compare and contrast the stories below.

Answering and Generating Comprehension Questions

Introduction

Having students answer comprehension questions is a tried-and-true teaching technique. If students know the questions before they read, they find a purpose for reading and a reason to personally connect to the text. Students benefit from being able to identify different types of questions because they will know where and how to look for answers.

Two basic categories of comprehension questions are *lower-order* and *higher-order*. Lower-order questions are factual, with answers that can be found directly in the text. Higher-order questions involve critical thinking; in other words, students must form their own opinions and then connect them to what is in the text in order to answer. Young students usually find these two categories sufficient. Older or more advanced students may benefit from dividing lower-order and higher-order into two additional subcategories as stated in the QAR method of questioning originated by Taffy Raphael in the 1980s (Raphael, T. E. (1986). Teaching Question Answer Relationships, revisited. *The Reading Teacher* 39 (6): 516-522.). Lower-order question subcategories can be *explicit* (right there) or *implicit* (think and search). Answers to explicit questions can be underlined in the text. Answers to implicit questions can be found in the text, but a student must be able to integrate sections of the entire book to find them. Below are examples of explicit and implicit questions from *Charlotte's Web* by E. B. White (HarperTrophy, 1974).

- Explicit question: How many goslings hatched? (seven)
- Implicit question: What did Charlotte do to keep Wilbur from being butchered? (She wrote slogans about him in her webs that made him famous.)

Higher-order questions can be further divided into *inductive* (author and reader) and *scriptal* (on your own). Inductive (author and reader) questions involve using the text to determine the author's implied meaning or intention; the answers are more complex than facts found in the text. Scriptal questions may require students to use their knowledge of the text as a backdrop, but they do not have to refer directly to anything in the text. Examples of inductive and scriptal questions from *Charlotte's Web* are below.

- Inductive question: Why did Charlotte decide to save Wilbur? (She saved Wilbur because she was kind and clever. She also liked Wilbur and wanted him to live a long life, even if she could not. Student answers will vary but are correct as long as they can be substantiated in the text.)
- Scriptal question: What would you have done to save Wilbur? (Answers will vary.)

After students have learned how to classify questions, teach them to generate questions. When students write comprehension questions, they have to think of the answers. This helps students grasp concepts in the text. Generating questions also encourages students to look for information throughout the text. When a question comes from you, students may focus on one part of the story, but when students have to write the questions, they may be motivated to look through the entire text to come up with ideas.

Comprehension Bingo

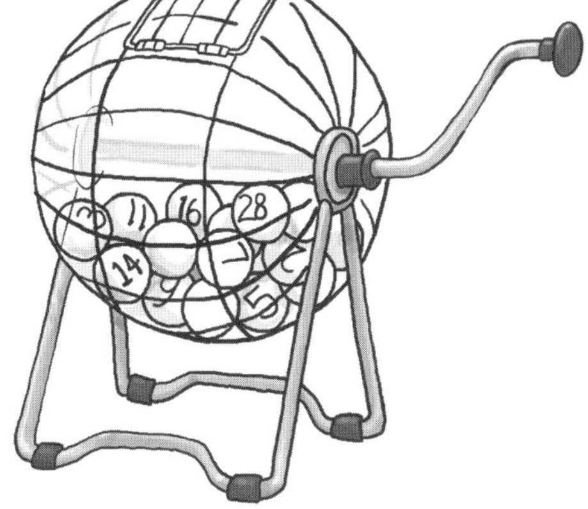

Use the programmable Bingo Card (page 36) to assess comprehension. Generate a class-created list of words from a current story or article so that all students will have the same answers on their Bingo Cards. For example, after reading *Charlotte's Web* by E. B. White (HarperTrophy, 1974) possible Bingo answers might be *Charlotte, Fern, Wilbur, farm, rat, Some Pig,* etc. Let students randomly fill in their cards with answers from the list. Then, write a master list of comprehension questions that can be answered by words and phrases on the first list. For example, a possible master list question might be *Who saved Wilbur's life?* (Each student should mark the space on her Bingo Card that says *Charlotte.*) Call out comprehension questions from the master list until a student has five answers in a row on her card. This game can also be used with informational text. Simply have students fill in their cards with facts, definitions, etc. As an alternative, have students fill in their Bingo Cards with questions and call out the answers.

Lower-Order Scavenger Hunt

Introduce lower-order questions with a scavenger hunt. Obtain several copies of a simple book that most students can read independently. Books that would work well with these questions are *The Grouchy Ladybug* by Eric Carle (HarperCollins, 1986), *Click, Clack, Moo: Cows That Type* by Doreen Cronin (Simon & Schuster, 2000), *Caps for Sale* by Esphyr Slobodkina (HarperCollins, 1987), *Flat Stanley* by Jeff Brown (HarperCollins, 1964), *Leo the Late Bloomer* by Robert Kraus (HarperCollins, 1994), or any other easy storybook in which the main character has a problem to solve. Read the book aloud. Assign students to groups of four and give each group a copy of the book and a copy of the Lower-Order Scavenger Hunt reproducible (page 37). Make sure that each group has at least one member who can read and write independently. Review the scavenger hunt questions as a class. Tell students to count off in their groups so that each group member has a number between one and four. At this point, tell member #1 in each group to take a copy of the book and the reproducible, find the answer to question #1 in Section A, and write it on a separate sheet of paper. If the student cannot read and write independently, allow the group member(s) who can read and write to help him. If the student has trouble finding the answer, let him consult other group members. After a few minutes, turn the classroom lights off and on quickly as a signal for member #1 in each group to pass the book and the reproducible to member #2. Repeat with the remaining group members, then let member #1 answer the first question in Section B. Pause before Section C and explain that, while these questions are still lower-order, the answers may require students to look in several places. When groups have completed all three sections, review the answers. Then, explain what about these questions makes them lower-order. (The answers can be found in the text.)

Name ______________________________________ *Comprehension Questions*

Bingo Card

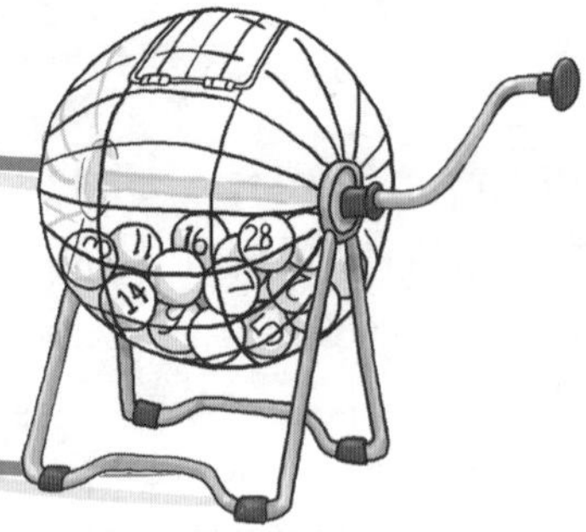

Name ____________________________________

Lower-Order Scavenger Hunt

When your teacher tells you to, answer the question in each section that matches your number. For example, if you are group member #1, answer the first question in each section. Use a separate sheet of paper to write the answers.

Section A

1. Is the main character a boy, girl, or animal?
2. What is the name of the main character?
3. Is the main character an animal or person?
4. Can you find and list a character that is not the main character?

Section B

1. Is the main character happy or sad at the beginning of the book?
2. What clues tell you how the main character is feeling?
3. Choose a character that is not the main character. What words or pictures does the author use to tell how this character feels?
4. Does something happen in the book to change how the main character feels?

Section C

1. What is the main event in the book?
2. What caused the main event to happen?
3. What did the characters do when the main event happened?
4. How does the story end?

Remember the Details

Demonstrate creating lower-order questions whose answers can be found in the text. As an example, read *Little Bunny's Sleepless Night* by Carol Roth (North-South Books, 2002). Ask some lower-order questions, such as, "Who did Little Bunny visit during the night? How did they keep him awake?" Write students' answers on the board. Remind students that the answers can be found in the book, so these are lower-order questions. Give each student one 6" x 9" (15 cm x 23 cm) and four 6" x 4 1/2" (15 cm x 11.5 cm) pieces of white construction paper. Have each student stack the four small pieces on top of the large piece of construction paper, then use two staples to attach the pages on the left side. On the bottom sheet of paper, direct each student to draw and color a bed so that the foot of the bed is underneath the smaller sheets of paper and the head extends so that it can be seen without opening the "book." Each student should also draw a picture of Little Bunny awake in the bed. On the top of each smaller piece of paper, have students draw the foot of the bed with a picture of an animal keeping Little Bunny awake. For example, the first page should show Squirrel. Because there is a picture of a bed on the bottom piece of paper, it should look like Squirrel is sitting on top of the bed. Beneath the animal on each page, students should write what the animal did. For example, students could write *Squirrel ate acorns in bed.* Have students finish their books by drawing all five animals that Little Bunny visited in the night and writing a sentence to tell how each animal kept Little Bunny awake. Let students look at the books to remember details and look for answers.

Deductive Reasoning

Answers to higher-order questions are not as obvious as answers to lower-order questions, and they require students to read two or three sentences and use deductive reasoning. Sometimes an answer is partly listed in the book and partly created by the student. As an example, read *I Will Never Not Ever Eat a Tomato* by Lauren Child (Candlewick Press, 2003). Then, ask, "How did Charlie get Lola to eat her vegetables?" Give each student a large paper plate. Encourage students to think about the story and use their own knowledge to answer the question. Have students write their responses on the paper plates. For the next question, ask, "Do you think Lola knows that tomatoes are not moonsquirters? Why?" Direct each student to turn his plate over and write the answer on the back of the plate. Allow each student to decorate his plate by drawing vegetables on it or by cutting out pictures of vegetables from magazines and gluing them to the plate. Punch a hole in the top of each plate. String a piece of yarn through each hole, knot the yarn, and hang several plates from a coat hanger to create a mobile. Repeat until all students' plates have been displayed.

Character Thoughts

Choose a book whose main character is a pig, such as *If You Give a Pig a Pancake* by Laura Joffe Numeroff (HarperCollins, 1998), *Perfect the Pig* by Susan Jeschke (Henry Holt, 1996), or *Olivia* by Ian Falconer (Simon & Schuster, 2000), to demonstrate an implicit lower-order question. Review the definition of lower-order questions. Explain that some lower-order questions have answers that are not quite as obvious but can still be figured out directly from the text. Read the book aloud. Then, select a page that contains an illustration of the main character. Ask students, "What do you think the main character is thinking in this picture?" Help students understand that the character's actions can help them make educated guesses about the character's thoughts. Have students write their responses in the thought bubble on the Character Thoughts reproducible (page 40). Have students write detailed responses from the character's point of view. To display the work, draw the face of a pig on pink bulletin board paper, cut it out, and post it on a bulletin board. Then, staple the thought bubbles around the pig to create a bulletin board titled "What Was This Pig Thinking?"

Create a Story from a Story

Show students that some stories do not have many words. Use a wordless picture book, such as *Tuesday* by David Wiesner (Houghton Mifflin, 1997). Show pictures from the book, provide paper, and direct each student to write a story that goes with the pictures. When students finish, have each student write three comprehension questions about the story on a separate piece of paper. Encourage students to write both lower- and higher-order questions. Direct students to turn over their papers and write the answers. Remind students that there may be multiple answers to some questions. For higher-order questions, have students write example answers and add the phrase *Answers may vary*. Assign partners and have them switch stories. After reading each other's stories, tell partners to ask their comprehension questions. Allow time for the author to reveal the answers. Compile the stories into a class book with each story followed by its matching comprehension questions page. Add a cover and the title *Tuesday Stories by Mr. Calhoun's Class*. Let students browse the book and answer the questions using their favorite strategies.

Character Thoughts

Think about the main character.
Write what the character is thinking in the thought bubble.

Clues Provide Answers

Explain that sometimes when readers have questions about text, the answers are easy to find, but sometimes, there are only hints about what the answers might be. When an author gives clues, it is up to the reader to figure out the answers. As an example, give each student a copy of the Beautiful Music reproducible (page 42) and read *Mole Music* by David McPhail (Henry Holt, 2001). At the pages listed below, stop and read the questions from the Beautiful Music reproducible. Have students use their own experiences and the author's words to write answers for each question. Schedule time for students to share their answers. Remember that because the questions are implicit, answers will vary.

Page 9 Why did the birds fly away? (The terrible sound of Mole's violin scared the birds away.)

Page 12 Why is there music coming up the tree? (The music is floating through the roots and up through the tree.)

Page 17 Does Mole ever play music for people? Who? (Yes. Mole plays for people above ground, but he does not realize it.)

Page 26 Did Mole's music change the world? How? (Yes. The music calmed two groups of people who were battling in a war. Mole stopped the war.)

Open-Ended Questions

Some activities require students to understand higher-order questions. The answers to these questions are not specifically found in the book but are open-ended. Students must use their life experiences and prior knowledge to come up with answers. Introduce *The Mysteries of Harris Burdick* by Chris Van Allsburg (Houghton Mifflin, 1996). This book has wonderful black-and-white illustrations with titles and picture captions. It is up to the reader to fill in the rest of the story using his higher-order thinking skills. Show the pages to the class and read the short text. Have students answer a higher-order question. Turn to one page and ask, "What happened in this story?" Remind students that there are no answers in the book. The answers come completely from their imaginations. Let a few students answer, then have each student select a page from the book and write or dictate a story about the picture. Assemble the stories into a class book. Add the title *The Mysteries of Room 141.* Allow volunteers to read their stories to the class.

Name ______________________________

Beautiful Music

Read the story *Mole Music*.
Write the answer to each question on the lines.

1. Why did the birds fly away? ______________________________

2. Why is there music coming up the tree? ______________________________

3. Does Mole ever play music for people? Who? ______________________________

4. Did Mole's music change the world? How? ______________________________

Trading Questions

Review the types of comprehension questions: a lower-order question can be answered from the text, while a higher-order question is either hinted at by the author or must be answered entirely by the reader. (See page 34 for more complete descriptions.) As an example, introduce *The Dinosaurs of Waterhouse Hawkins* by Barbara Kerley (Scholastic, 2001). Tell students that Waterhouse Hawkins built models of dinosaurs. Give each student a copy of the Trading Questions reproducible (page 44). On the reproducible, point out the dinosaur with definitions of lower- and higher-order questions. Have students cut out the dinosaurs and glue them to craft sticks. As you read the first part of the book (*The First Age: London*) have students answer a higher-order question in which they will have to think about the author's intentions, such as, "What steps did Waterhouse take to build a dinosaur?" Then, have students review their definitions on the paper dinosaurs and think of higher-order questions about the same section. As each student thinks of a question, have her raise her dinosaur. Let students trade questions back and forth, then repeat the procedure with the second and third sections of the book. Each time a student asks a question, have her identify whether it is higher-order or lower-order.

Name That Question

Give students practice thinking of questions with this nonbook exercise. Bring several children's magazines to class. Let students flip through the magazines. Allow each student to cut out one article or story he finds interesting and read it. Then, have him generate five questions about the article or story. Also, have each student answer her questions and designate whether each question is lower-order or higher-order on a separate piece of paper. Ask students to trade articles and questions with classmates. Let classmates answer the questions and identify which types of questions they are, then return the papers to the owners. Have students compare their classmates' answers and identification of question types with their own. Review any discrepancies about question types with each pair of students and be sure to note that answers may be different with higher-order questions.

Trading Questions

Cut out the dinosaur. Glue it to a craft stick. Listen to your teacher's directions.

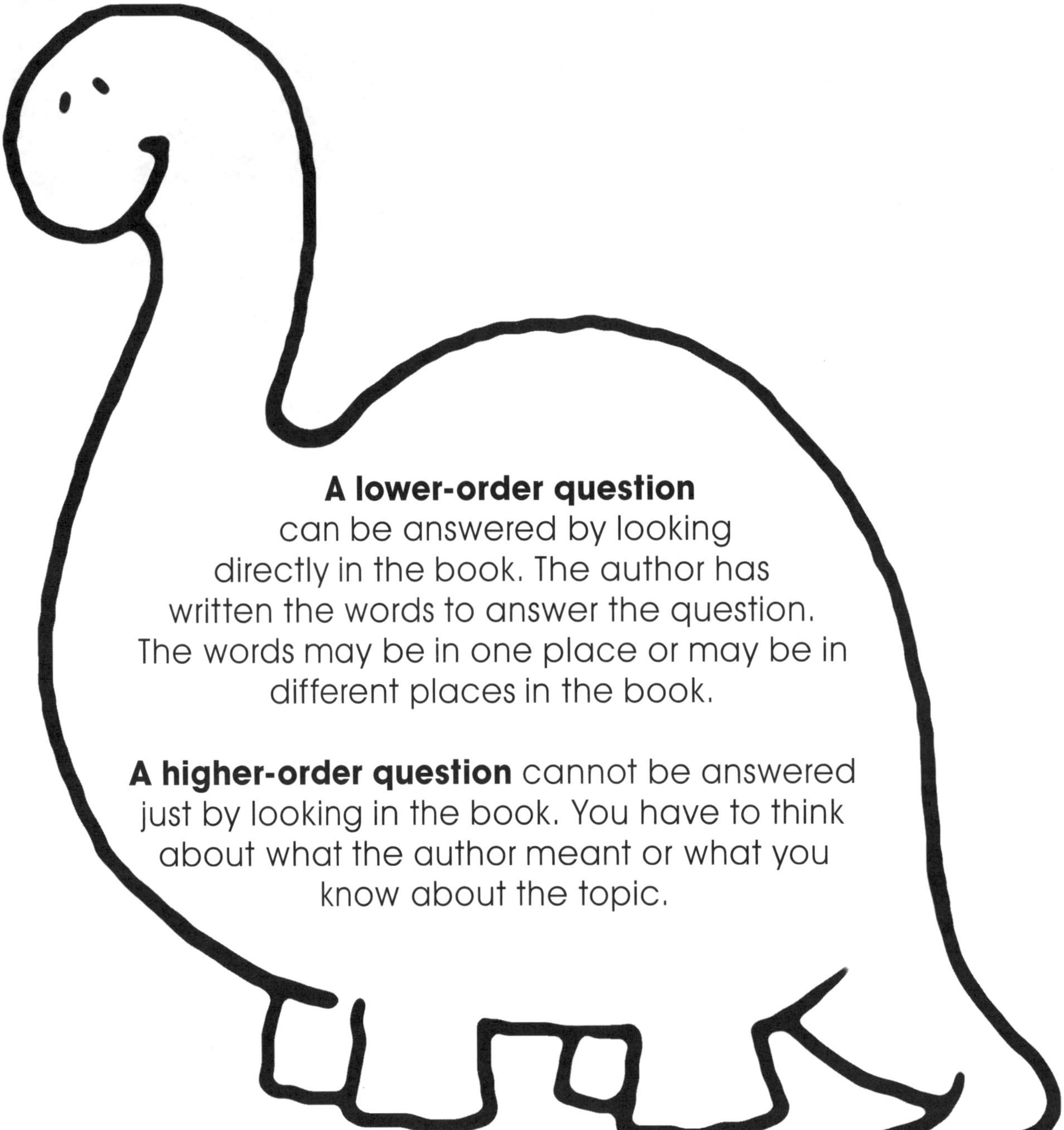

A lower-order question can be answered by looking directly in the book. The author has written the words to answer the question. The words may be in one place or may be in different places in the book.

A higher-order question cannot be answered just by looking in the book. You have to think about what the author meant or what you know about the topic.

Student-Created Center

As students become more comfortable with generating and answering questions, increase their responsibility while reinforcing the value of creating comprehension questions. Direct each student to select a favorite book from the class library that she can read independently. Have students read their books carefully so that they remember the stories. Then, direct each student to write three questions about her book on a piece of paper. Encourage students to use both types of questions. After students have written the questions, have them write the answers on separate pieces of paper. Remind students that some questions may have multiple answers. For higher-order questions, students should write example answers, but they should also add *Answers may vary.* Have each student fold her papers and place them in separate envelopes. Have each student write the title of the book on the outside of the question envelope and attach the envelope to the inside back cover of the book with a paper clip. Group books of similar reading levels together. Keep the answer envelopes at your desk. At center time, place the books at a center. Make sure the center group's reading ability matches the level of the books. Direct each student to read a book and answer the questions at the end on a separate piece of paper. Provide the answer envelopes for students to check their answers.

Teacher for a Day

Have each student be the teacher for a day and conduct a reading lesson. Let each student choose a favorite picture book from the classroom or school library. (If students prefer to select chapter books, limit the lessons to one chapter.) Tell students to reread the books independently. Then, have each student write three comprehension questions about his book. Encourage students to write both lower-order and higher-order questions. If a student is not able to write both types because of the style of the book, allow him to use only one type of question. Make sure students write the answers to the questions. Remind students that there may be multiple answers to a question; for these questions, have students write example answers. For higher-order questions, have students add the phrase *Answers may vary.* When students are ready, schedule time for the "guest teachers" to present their books over two weeks. Each day, have the "teacher" read his book aloud and guide the class in a discussion by asking his comprehension questions. Make sure the "teachers" also share the answers to the questions.

Book Week

Celebrate books by announcing a class Book Week. Select five books you would like to read aloud. Copy the Bookmarks reproducible (page 47) onto card stock to make bookmark prizes. Assign students to five groups. Give each group one book and give each student one index card. Have the strongest reader in each group read the book to the other group members or have group members take turns. Then, direct each group member to write a comprehension question about his book. Encourage groups to create various questions, both easy and difficult. Have each student write a question and answer on the same side of an index card. Remind students that there may be multiple answers to higher-order questions; for these, have students write example answers and add the phrase *Answers may vary*. Each day during Book Week, read one of the five books. After reading the book, read one group question. Call on a student from a different group for the answer. If the student is correct, give her a bookmark or another small prize. If a student answers incorrectly, ask another student for an answer. Ask the remaining questions for that book and reward correct answers. Repeat the routine each day of Book Week and provide an opportunity for each student to win a bookmark. On the final day, allow students to decorate their bookmarks by decorating the illustrations, punching out the holes, and adding yarn tassels.

Story Time JEOPARDY!®

Play a question game with students but instead of asking questions and having students give you the answers, give students an answer and let volunteers think of questions. First read a book, then say an answer. Have students think of as many different questions as possible that have that answer. For example, if you read a version of *Goldilocks and the Three Bears*, you could say the answer, "Goldilocks." Questions that match that answer could be, "Who was the main character of the book? Who broke into the bears' home? and Who ate the bears' porridge?" Encourage students to think of a variety of questions. For example, if the answer is "Papa Bear," an explicit question that matches that answer could be, "Whose chair was too big?" An inductive question could be, "Which bear is the grumpiest?" A scriptal question could be, "If you could be any of the bears, which one would you be?" (Note that these questions might not work for all versions of *Goldilocks and the Three Bears*.) When you finish, let students take turns supplying questions for a different book.

Name ______________________

Bookmarks

Cut apart the bookmarks and use them as prizes.

Class Comprehension

Divide the class into four heterogeneous groups. Assign a type of comprehension question to each group. Either assign two groups lower-order questions and two groups higher-order questions, or assign each group a different type (explicit, implicit, inductive, or scriptal), as defined on page 34. Read a story aloud that will be easy for students to generate questions about. Then, give each group three index cards and a piece of bulletin board paper. Use a different color paper for each group. Have each group work together to create three of their type of questions. Direct students to write each question on the front of an index card and the answer on the back. The answers for the inductive and scriptal questions will vary, but have the groups give possible answers. Tell each group to write the type of question on the bulletin board paper. Have them tape the index cards to the bulletin board paper by the tops of the cards so that they can lift the cards to see the answers on the backs. Hang each completed bulletin board paper at the front of the classroom. Challenge the class to see how many questions they can answer correctly. Read each group's questions and call on students from other groups to answer them. If the answers to the inductive and scriptal questions seem plausible, count them as correct. Keep track of how many questions the whole class answers correctly.

Comprehending through Reporting

Have students use the process of generating questions to conduct research about a favorite topic. For example, for a topic about animals, let each student choose one animal. Give each student a copy of the Animal Report reproducible (page 49). Tell each student to write the name of the animal she is researching on the reproducible. Then, have her think of five areas about the animal that she would like to research. Direct students to write these areas in the form of questions. For example, a student may write questions like *What does a giraffe eat? Where does a giraffe live?* and *Would a giraffe make a good pet?* Schedule time for students to research the animals. Tell students to write their answers below their questions on the reproducibles. When students complete their research, have them draw pictures of their animals on the backs of the reproducibles. Then, have each student use the information to help her create a poster about her animal. On the poster, have each student include pictures and at least three interesting facts about her animal. Schedule time for students to share their information. Direct students to hang their posters, read their questions, and reveal the answers to the class.

Name ______________________________

Animal Report

Choose an animal. Write five questions you want to answer. Find the answers to the questions. Draw a picture of your animal on the back of this paper.

Type of animal: ______________________________

1. Question: ______________________________

   Answer: ______________________________

   ____

2. Question: ______________________________

   Answer: ______________________________

   ____

3. Question: ______________________________

   Answer: ______________________________

   ____

4. Question: ______________________________

   Answer: ______________________________

   ____

5. Question: ______________________________

   Answer: ______________________________

   ____

Question-and-Answer Board

Playing games is an enjoyable way for students to practice generating and answering questions. Let students use enlarged copies of the Game Board reproducible (page 51) and index cards to create games. Have students color the board and add a few directions, such as *Move up one space, Lose a turn, Move back two spaces*, etc. Allow students to program their Game Boards to fit the theme of the particular book or topic being read. For example, when reading about reptiles, students can decorate their Game Boards and question cards with reptile-themed illustrations. Or, have students decorate the Game Board with general illustrations in order to reuse throughout the year. If possible, laminate the Game Boards for durability. Then, have students generate questions based on the reading and write each question on a separate index card. Tell students to include the answers on the cards and to check their answers carefully to ensure they are accurate. Students may want to decorate the blank sides of the question cards, as well. Then, pair students. Have students use buttons, coins, or squares of colorful construction paper as game pieces. Instruct students to take turns asking each other questions from their own stacks of question cards. If a player answers a question correctly, he may move one space on the board. If the player lands on a space that has directions, such as, *Move back one space*, have him do that, as well. If the player answers the question incorrectly, his game piece should remain where it is while the next player takes a turn. The first player to reach the finish wins.

Question Review

Review the kinds of comprehension questions: lower-order and higher-order. Remind students that knowing which type of question is being asked will help them find the answer. Then, use this exercise to assess their understanding of the concepts. Select a book to read aloud to students, such as *And to Think That I Saw It on Mulberry Street* by Dr. Seuss (Random House, 1972). After reading the book, review and model an example of a lower-order question. For this book, an example could be, "What did the boy really see on Mulberry Street?" or "What was the first new animal that the boy imagined pulling the cart?" Have students think of examples of lower-order questions about the book. Then, call on students to share their questions. Write students' responses on the board. Repeat this process with higher-order questions. For this book, an example could be, "What do you think the boy's father would have said if the boy described the imaginary things he saw on Mulberry Street?" or "Why did the boy want to impress his father?" Discuss students' responses. Repeat this process with other books and provide opportunities for each student to dictate a question.

Name ______________________________

Game Board

Color the game board below.
On index cards, write questions and answers
from your reading. To play the game, take turns asking and answering questions. Move ahead one space for each right answer. The first player to reach the finish wins!

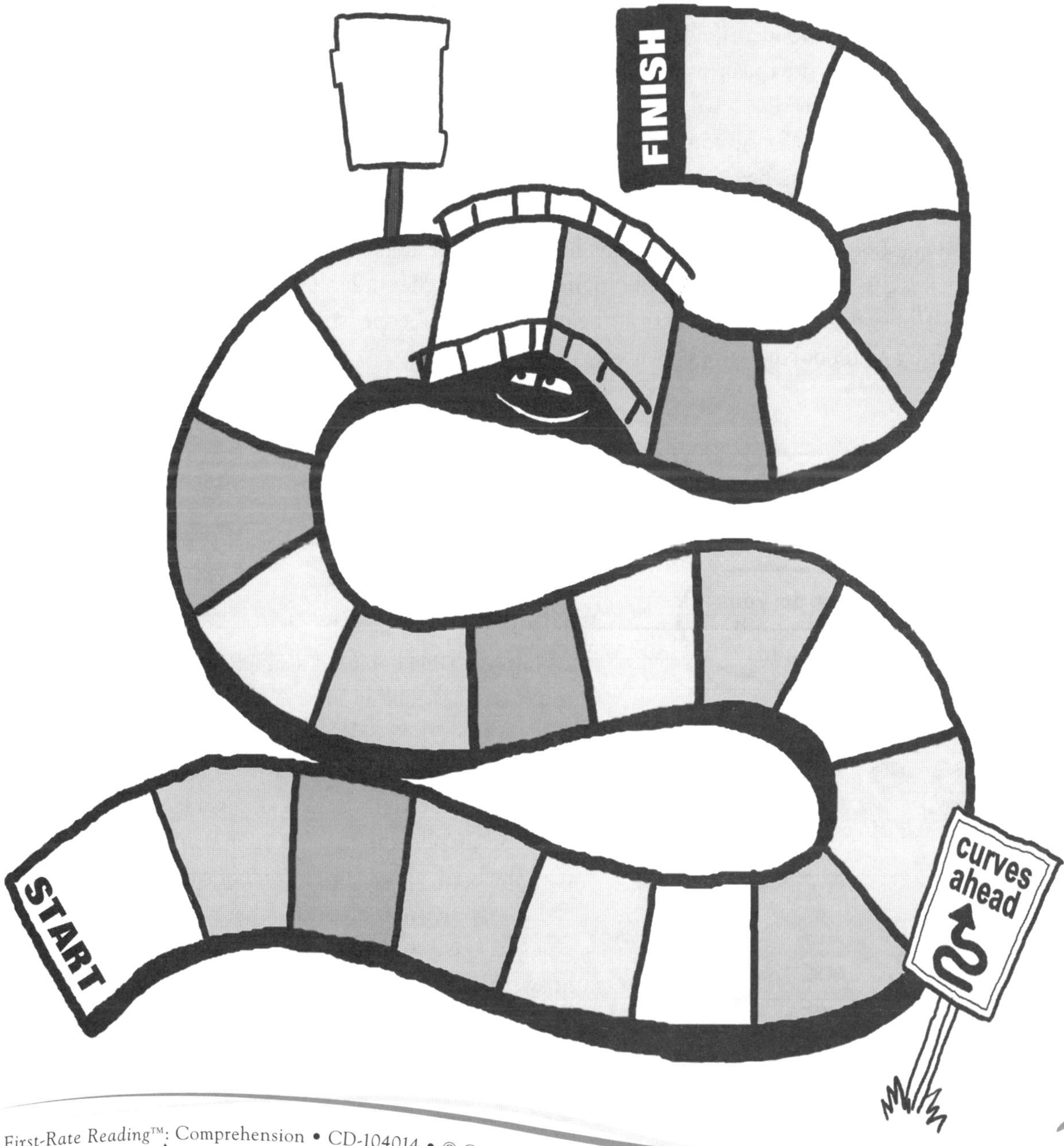

The Great Librarian Challenge

Ask the school librarian if she is willing to participate in The Great Librarian Challenge. If so, ask her to identify her favorite book at your students' grade level. (She may want to reread it a few times before the challenge!) To run the challenge, read the librarian's favorite book with students. Then, give one copy of The Great Librarian Challenge reproducible (page 53) to each student. Have each student cut out the form and fold it on the solid line so that it looks like a little book, then unfold it. On the left side, have each student write a question about the book in hopes of stumping the librarian. Encourage each student to identify her question as lower-order or higher-order. Have her write the answer on the right side. For each question that has multiple answers, have the student write an example answer and add the phrase *Answer may vary*. Have each student write her name on the "cover." Then, have students refold their completed question forms and place them in a paper bag. Schedule a time to go to the library. Take the questions to the library and start The Great Librarian Challenge. Pull out a question to have a student ask the librarian. If the librarian is correct, she gets a point. If she is incorrect, the class gets a point. When the librarian answers a higher-order question, give her a point if her answer makes sense. Whoever has the most points at the end of the challenge wins. Reward students and the librarian for participating with bookmarks or certificates of participation.

Chapter Book Questions

Obtain multiple copies of a simple chapter book. Divide the class into small groups. Assign each group one chapter from the book and give them a copy of the book. Have each group read their assigned chapter and write three questions as well as possible answers to the questions. Collect the questions and answers. Then, read the book aloud. At the end of each chapter, ask the comprehension questions that were written for that chapter. Have students who did not write the questions answer them.

The Great Librarian Challenge

Listen to the story. Cut out
the book. Write a question for the librarian on
the left side. Write the answer on the right side. Fold the book in half.

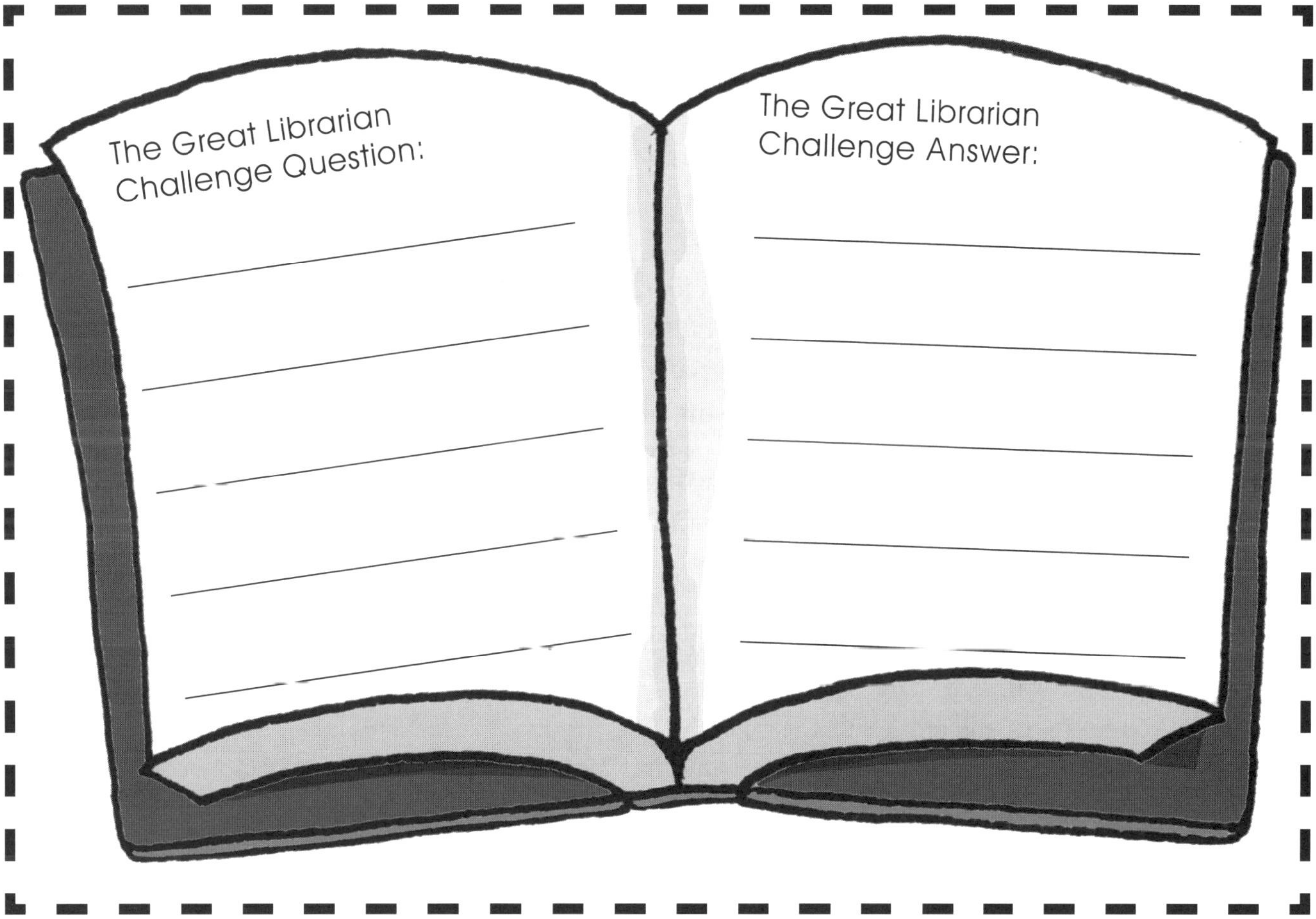

Recognizing Story Structure

Introduction

Story structure refers to the way a story is organized. Identifying the plot, sequence, characters, problem, and resolution of a story increases student comprehension. Teaching children about story structure helps them remember stories better, understand them more deeply, and have greater appreciation for the content.

Chain of Events

Cut pieces of different-colored construction paper into strips about 1" (2.5 cm) wide. Give each student strips of one color for his chain of events. Read aloud a book that has a clear sequence. Explain that every story has a certain order, which is called the *sequence*. Explain to students that when they understand the sequence of a story, they can remember and understand the story better. As you read, have students pay special attention to the sequence of events in the story. Then, ask what happened first. Have each student write his response on a strip of construction paper, then tape or staple the paper into a ring. Ask what happened next. Instruct each student to write the next event on a second strip of paper then loop the second paper strip through the first one and staple or tape it into a ring. Continue to ask, "What happened next?" until you get to the end of the story. Have each student write his answer, add a link, and keep the links in the same order of the story until he reaches the end. Have each student write his final loop, then connect students' chains together. Since each student has only one color in his chain, it will be clear where one student's chain ends and another student's chain begins. Hang the paper chains from the ceiling. Let students complete this activity independently with other books.

Plot Checklist

Explain that every story has a structure. There are *characters* (the main people or animals in a story), a *setting* (where the story takes place), and usually a *problem* and a *resolution*. Give students an example of a problem and its resolution from a familiar class book. Continue the discussion by stating that after the resolutions, most plots have *conclusions*. When students understand these parts, it is easier for them to understand new books. Direct each student to select a book she can read independently. Give each student a copy of the Plot Checklist reproducible (page 55). Tell students that the reproducible is a checklist for recognizing these story parts. Have students read their stories and use the checklist to identify the various components. For example, students should write the main characters' names and then put checks in front of *Characters* on the list. Then, they should write the settings and put checks next to *Setting* on the list, and so on. Have students continue until they find all of the structural elements.

Name ______________________

Plot Checklist

Read the story. Identify parts of the plot. Write them below and check them off as you find them.

☐ Book Title: ______________________

☐ Characters—the main people or animals in a story: ______________________

____

____

☐ Setting—where the story takes place: ______________________

____

☐ Problem—what is wrong in the story: ______________________

____

____

☐ Resolution—how the problem is solved: ______________________

____

____

☐ Conclusion—what happens at the end of the story: ______________________

____

____

Plot Dioramas

Ask students and colleagues to donate empty shoe boxes. Explain that each story has a beginning, middle, and end. In the beginning, the characters are introduced, the setting is described, and a plot begins. The main action of the story happens in the middle. In the end, the story and any loose ends are wrapped up. Give an example by using a familiar story, such as *Goldilocks and the Three Bears*. Have students explain what happens in the story. When they finish, explain that in the beginning of the story, Goldilocks (the main character) finds a small house in the forest (the setting). In the middle of the story, Goldilocks tries out the bears' porridge, chairs, and beds. (Tell students that you are summarizing when you identify the middle of the story; you do not tell every detail, just the main events.) At the end of the story, the three bears discover Goldilocks in Baby Bear's bed. She wakes up, is scared, and runs away. Divide the class into groups of three. Have each group select a book that they can read or assign a book to each group. Explain that one student in each group should make a diorama showing the beginning of the story, another student should make a diorama of the main event in the middle of the story, and the third student in the group should make a diorama of what happened at the end of the story. Have each group read their book. Provide three shoe boxes and art supplies for each group. Have students place their completed dioramas in order of beginning, middle, and end. Allow each group to explain their dioramas.

Domino Effect

Demonstrate the "domino effect" for students by standing several dominoes in a row and pushing the first one to make the others fall. Explain that the events in a story are like dominoes; they go in a certain order, and each event can affect what happens to the next event. Ask, "When you knock over dominoes, how do they fall? Does the first one fall, then the fifth one, then back to the second one, then the seventh one?" Students should answer that they fall in order. Tell students that the same is true in a story. First one event happens, causing the second event to happen, then the third, and so on. This is called the *story sequence*. Assign students to four or five small groups. Read a story aloud. Have students in each group work together to figure out the sequence of the story. Give each group several index cards. Ask, "What happened first in the story? Then, what happened? What happened next?" Have students write each event on an index card until they come to the end of the story. Ask students to number the cards to keep them in order. Next, give each group one domino for each card. Direct each student to roll a small piece of tape so that both sides are sticky, then place it on the flat side of the domino. Have each student tape the card to the domino. The bottom of each card should be even with or slightly higher than the bottom of the domino. Have students carefully place the domino cards in order of the events written on them and close enough so that they will hit each other when they fall. Have a student in each group read the cards aloud, showing the sequence of the story. Then, direct the groups to knock down the domino cards to illustrate the importance of sequencing a story.

Story Sequence

Help students understand plot by writing the sequence of a story. Choose a story with strong sequential elements, such as *The Great Gracie Chase: Stop That Dog!* by Cynthia Rylant (Scholastic, 2001). Read the book aloud, then give each student a copy of the Story Sequence reproducible (page 58) to help students organize the plot of the story. Have students write the title and author in the first square. Then, have students identify the main characters in the second square. In the third square, tell students to describe the setting. In the fourth square, have students write what happened first in the story. In the fifth square, direct students to write what happened in the middle of the story. In the sixth square, have students write how that problem was solved. In the last square, tell students to write what happened on the last page. Review student responses when the class is finished. For additional practice, let students use the reproducible to organize other stories' plots.

Cooperative Retelling

Identifying the beginning, middle, and end of a story helps students remember and understand the story better. Have students work cooperatively to tell the beginning, middle, and end of one of their favorite stories. Be sure to schedule enough time for group planning, in-class reading, and discussions. Divide the class into groups of three. Instruct each group to decide who will be responsible for retelling the beginning, middle, and end. Have each group select a book that the class has already read so as not to give away the endings of any new books. Explain that when a student tells the beginning, she should identify the title, characters, setting, and how the story begins. For the middle of the story, a student should describe the major action and main events. The retelling of the end of the story should include how the action or problem was resolved and what happened on the last page. Allow time for students to practice retelling the stories. When groups are ready, call one group to the front of the classroom. Have group members stand in a row in order of the events they are retelling and proceed to retell the story. After each group's presentation, ask other students if they agree with the way the group described the beginning, middle, and end of the story. If not, ask the audience what they would change. When all groups have had turns, reread the stories aloud to allow students to think about any events they may have forgotten.

Name ________________________________

Story Sequence

Answer the questions below.

Book Title and Author

____

____

Who are the main characters?

____

____

What is the setting?

____

____

What happened first in the story?

____

____

What happened in the middle of the story?

____

____

How was the problem solved?

____

____

What happened on the last page?

____

____

The Book Police

Tell students that they are going to become "Book Police" as they investigate the plot of a book by answering important questions. Give each student a copy of The Book Police reproducible (page 60). Allow students to select books they can read independently. Explain that police officers write reports about crimes or incidents they investigate. Students will have an opportunity to conduct their own investigations about the plots of books and take reports of incidents that happen in the stories. Have students read their books. Then, read each question and have students identify the main characters where the report says Suspects' Names. Next, have students describe the settings. Then, ask students to describe how the stories started (the beginning, or introduction) and the main actions (climaxes) of the stories. Finally, have students tell about the conclusions. Post the completed reports on a bulletin board titled "Room 305's Most Wanted."

Flip Book

Reinforce the idea that a story is told in a certain sequence. Students will understand and remember a story if they remember its sequence. First, provide an example of a flip book—a book with sequenced cartoons drawn on one side of the pages that appear to "move" when the pages are flipped rapidly. As an example, read *The Tin Forest* by Helen Ward (Puffin, 2003). Prompt students to think about the book's sequence. Ask volunteers to tell how the tin forest became a real forest. Then, give each student several unlined index cards. On the first card, tell each student to write the title and author. Have each student turn over the first card like she is opening a book. On the back of the first card, direct each student to write what happened first in the book and number this page 1. Have her write the number *1* in the lower left corner. On the next card, tell each student to illustrate what happened first in the story. When finished with the illustration, have each student turn over the illustration card again like a book page. On the back of the illustration page, have each student write what happened next in the story and number that page 2. Next, have each student illustrate her writing on the next card, and so on, until she reaches the end of the story. Direct students to mix up their cards and reread them. Ask, "Does the story make sense when all of the cards are out of order?" When students answer that the story no longer makes sense, have them reorder the cards and staple them together on the left sides to create mini-books. Students may be able to see the sequence illustrated if they hold their thumbs on the edges of their books and quickly flip the pages. All of the pictures should blend to show the main points of *The Tin Forest*.

Name ___________________________

The Book Police

Read a story. Write a police report about the story.

Suspects' Names (Main Characters)

Location (Setting)

How did this story begin?

What was the main action in this story?

How did the story end?

Dramatic Retelling

By retelling the sequence or order of a book, students will remember the details and appreciate the book even more. Introduce and read *King Bidgood's in the Bathtub* by Audrey Wood (Harcourt Brace, 1985). While reading, direct students to pay special attention to the sequence in the story. Write the following names of the main characters on the board: *the page*, *the king*, *the knight*, *the queen*, *the duke*, and *the court* (which is made up of several people). Mix up the order so that students are not sure which character appears first in the story. Then, divide the class into groups of at least six students. Assign characters or direct each student in the group to select a different character. The court may contain as many as four students. Provide art supplies and direct each student to draw her character's picture onto a craft stick to make a stick puppet. Instruct groups to practice retelling the story with their puppets. Make sure students understand that the order of their characters' appearances needs to be the same order as the story. Have each student hold up her puppet and tell her character's part of the story. The words do not have to be exact in the retelling, but the sequence of events does. Schedule time for each group to perform a retelling.

Silly Story Lines Stick

Help students understand the meaning of the word *plot* by reading a fun story. As an example, read a book that contains a pie somewhere in the story line, such as *Sweet Dream Pie* by Audrey Wood (Scholastic, 2002), *More Pies!* by Robert Munsch (Scholastic, 2003), *Amelia Bedelia* by Peggy Parish (HarperCollins, 2003), or *I Know an Old Lady Who Swallowed a Pie* by Alison Jackson (Puffin, 2002). Explain that students will answer some questions about the story's plot. Give each student a copy of the Easy as Pie reproducible (page 62). There is a question about the plot in each section of the pie. Direct students to think about the story and answer each question. Have students write their responses in the different pie sections. Review the following questions with students: *Who are the main characters? What did they want? What happened? How was it fixed?* When students have answered the questions, review the answers. Have students cut out the pies and lightly color them to look like their favorite kinds of pies. Display the pies on a bulletin board titled "Easy as Pie!" Use the Easy as Pie reproducible to help students practice identifying the plots of other stories.

Name ______________________________

Recognizing Story Structure

Easy as Pie

Write your answers to the questions on the pieces of pie.

Summarizing

Introduction

Summarizing means being able to read text, figure out what is important (and not important) in that text, compress this information into a few words, and retell the information. By learning how to summarize, students can identify main ideas, distinguish important information from unimportant information, and better remember what they read.

Concrete Main Idea Identification

Help students understand the concept of main idea using concrete objects. Show students a pencil, an eraser, loose-leaf paper, a ruler, and a box of crayons. Ask students to explain the main idea of these objects (school supplies). Discuss how they were able to infer this main idea, what clues they used, etc. Repeat with other items, such as a party hat, balloon, candle, and card (birthday items); a fork, spoon, dish, napkin, and cup (eating utensils); etc. Extend the activity by having students bring in items that represent main ideas. Next, move to nonfiction. Choose an easy chapter book about a nonfiction topic, such as weather. Read the chapter titles aloud without revealing the title or cover of the book. Ask students to name the main idea of the book. Then, read one of the chapters without revealing its title and ask students to name the main idea of the chapter. Finally, try the same exercise with a very simple book, such as *No, David!* by David Shannon (Scholastic, 1998). Ask students to name the main idea (no matter how naughty little David is, his mother still loves him). Repeat with a nonfiction book, such as *The Man Who Walked Between the Towers* by Mordicai Gerstein (Roaring Brook, 2003). Discuss what is different about finding the main ideas in fiction and nonfiction books. Which do students think is easier?

Distinguishing Details

Explain that a key skill in understanding how to summarize a text is being able to distinguish important information from unimportant information. Although small details add interest to a story, students should look for the most important information when summarizing. Write the statements from the Important Announcement reproducible (page 64) on sentence strips and display the strips. Tell students that you have a list of morning announcements from an imaginary principal. Some of the announcements are very important while others are not important at all. Have volunteers read the list of statements. (Remind students that these announcements are not real, they are just made up.) Distribute the Important Announcement reproducible. As you read the announcements aloud, have students circle the most important statements on their lists. Then, have students share the statements they selected as the most important. Ask students why they considered those statements to be the most important ones.

Important Announcement

Circle the announcements that are important enough for the principal to share with the entire school.

1. I brought a peanut butter sandwich for lunch today.

2. School will be canceled next Friday. Do not come to school next Friday.

3. I wore brown shoes today.

4. The P. E. teacher forgot to hang a poster.

5. The whole school will go on a field trip tomorrow to the video game factory. You may only go if you have a permission slip. Bring your permission slip tomorrow.

6. The music teacher sneezed two days ago.

7. The school secretary is cleaning out her files.

8. A first grader checked out a book from the library yesterday.

9. There is a major test tomorrow. If you fail, you will not move up to the next grade.

10. Mrs. Smith is using new chalk today.

Translation Please

Review summarizing skills and discuss the value of putting information into your own words. Explain that summarizing means that students should talk about the book but should sound like they normally speak. For example, ask if they ever say, "Let's partake in some delicious refueling at noon." Instead, they probably say, "Let's eat lunch." The words mean the same thing, but they were changed to sound more like the way students speak. Students should do the same thing when summarizing. Give students some practice changing text into their own words. Read the following passage: *The object of this lesson is to strengthen your ability to summarize text and make sure that you learn new skills for the purpose of understanding material that you read. At this point in time, it would be my choice for you to take out your paper and writing utensils to begin recording information in your journals.* Stop occasionally to help students translate phrases into their own words. Give several students opportunities to answer.

Beginning, Middle, End Summary

Help students use the beginning, middle, and end strategies they have learned to summarize a story. Use a favorite story to give students practice summarizing the beginning, middle, and end of a story. Give each student a copy of the Beginning-Middle-End reproducible (page 66). As you reread a familiar story to the class, have students use the top portion of the reproducible to make short notes and draw simple illustrations about what takes place at the beginning, middle, and end of the story. Have students write short phrases about each section of the story. Explain that when students tell the beginning, they should identify the characters, setting, and how the story begins. Next, have students describe the major action and main events. Finally, the end of the story should include notes about how the action was resolved and what happened at the end. After you finish reading the story, have each student rewrite his summary notes in paragraph form at the bottom of the page. Instruct each student to write at least one sentence about each section of the story.

Name ______________________________

Beginning-Middle-End

Summarizing is easier when you focus on the main events. On the lines below, write about events that happened at the beginning, middle, and end of the story. Then, use your notes to write a summary.

Beginning: ______________________________

____

____

____

Middle: ______________________________

____

____

____

End: ______________________________

____

____

____

Use your notes to write a summary of the story: ______________________________

____

____

____

____

____

10 Words or Less

Explain that when readers summarize a story or book, they take a lot of information and squeeze it down to just a few important words. Demonstrate by reading a paragraph aloud. Then, summarize the paragraph in 10 words or less. Hold up one finger for every word. (Emphasize that you are not counting syllables, but whole words.) Read another paragraph. Assign students to pairs and have each student summarize the paragraph by repeating the important information to his partner in 10 words or less. As Partner A summarizes the paragraph, Partner B should hold up one finger for each word and tell if Partner A was able to summarize in 10 words or less. Remind students that summarizing takes a little practice, then read another paragraph and have partners switch roles. Continue alternating between partners until each student can easily summarize a paragraph in 10 words.

In Your Own Words

When students summarize, they should look for important information, make it shorter, and change the words to sound like they are speaking (not the author). Model this skill by reading a brief passage from a book. Summarize the passage, making the summary sound like the way you speak. Next, give each student a copy of the In Your Own Words reproducible (page 68). Direct students to read each statement on the left. (For younger students, read the statements aloud.) Tell students to think about what the statement means and write how they would say it on the lines. Ask students to share their answers. Then, for extra practice, have a volunteer summarize what she did during this activity!

In Your Own Words, Part 2

Use a real event to help students compare and contrast their summarization skills. Before a class party or field trip, tell students that you want them to summarize the event afterwards. After the event, assign students to small groups and tell them to write summaries of the event. Instruct each group to write only five sentences about the event. After students finish writing, reconvene as a class to share the summaries. As each group shares a summary, write their five sentences on a separate piece of chart paper. When all groups have shared their summaries, talk with the class about what was most difficult about the assignment. Was it hard to find enough information or did they have too much? Was it necessary to leave out important details? Ask a volunteer to identify what details were repeated in most summaries. Do students agree that these were the most important details?

In Your Own Words

Read the sentences.
Write how you would say the same information on the lines next to the sentences.

1. My deepest apologies, but I cannot attend your birthday gathering. ______________________

2. Perhaps you would like to join me at my house this sunny afternoon. ______________________

3. I truly enjoy exercising my muscles for fun on the grassy field outside. ______________________

4. Would you consider showing a film in class today? ______________________

5. Your friendship brings me the utmost happiness. ______________________

Book Jacket Summaries

Book jackets often contain summaries of books. Explain that students can read the summaries to help them decide if they want to read the books. Have students practice summarizing by creating book jacket summaries for books from the class library. Direct each student to choose a favorite book that he can read independently. Give each student a piece of construction paper or bulletin board paper. Instruct students to wrap the books in the paper to make book jackets. First, have each student place his closed book in the middle of the paper and fold the paper around the book. Have each student cut notches in the top and bottom of the paper where it meets the spine, then fold the sides of the paper around the front and back covers. Instruct each student to close the book with the jacket on to make sure that the jacket is large enough to fit. After the jackets are folded, have each student write the title of the book and the author on the front cover. Next, direct each student to read his book. Have him consolidate the important information in the book into two or three sentences. Then, have each student retell the information in his own words by writing a book summary on the back of the book jacket. Store the books (with the jackets) in the class library. Encourage students to choose their next books to read by reading the jackets.

Charting Summaries

Review the three parts of summarizing with students. First, they have to figure out which information is important and which information is not important. When they summarize, they are only telling the most important information of the story. Next, they should condense the most important information into a few sentences (squeeze the important information into a few words). The last step is to take the condensed version and rewrite it in their own words. Model this process using a transparency of the Summary Chart reproducible (page 70). Read a short book aloud. Record your answers on the transparency as you "think out loud" to figure out the important information from the story. Let students hear your thought process. Write the important information in the first column. Write the condensed version in the middle column. Finally, change the words to sound more like the way you speak but keep the same meaning. Write this final version in the last column. Use copies of the Summary Chart reproducible to give students guided practice with the same process. Read a book aloud or have students read independently. Have students complete summaries using the Summary Chart.

Name ________________________________

Summary Chart

Read a book. Complete a summary by filling in each column.

Book Title: ________________________________

Important Information	The Shorter Version	My Own Words

Smaller Versions

Select a short chapter book to read or one that students can read independently. One possibility is a selection from the *Frog and Toad* series by Arnold Lobel (HarperTrophy). Have students create smaller versions of the original text. Give each student a copy of the Smaller Version reproducible (page 72). Each day, read one chapter aloud. After reading, tell students to choose the important information in the chapter. Direct students to shorten the information into a few sentences and write that information in their own words on the reproducibles. Each day, encourage students to reread their previous chapter summaries to remember details about the story, then read a new chapter and have students write summaries on the reproducibles. When you finish the book, have students reread their chapter summaries and write short summaries of the entire book on separate pieces of paper. Have students cut out their squares, assemble the pages into mini-books, and staple the mini-books along the left sides. Tell students that they have written smaller versions (in both words and page size) of the book. When closing the lesson, explain that summarizing the chapters helped students remember details about the books and understand them better.

Now Playing: Posters That Summarize

Sometimes movie studios use posters to advertise their movies. A movie poster may include a summary that helps people decide if they want to see the movie. Have students apply this idea to their favorite books. Direct each student to choose a favorite book from the class or school library. Allow time for students to read their books. Have each student write a book summary. Students should combine the important information into one or two sentences, then rewrite the shorter versions in their own words. Give each student a large piece of white construction paper. Have each student write the book's title and the author on the poster. Direct students to use markers or crayons to illustrate their book posters before adding their summaries. Then, have students add the summaries to their posters. (You may want them to write the summaries in pencil before going over the words with markers.) Decorate the class library with the posters. The next time a student asks you to suggest a good book, have her read the posters.

Name ______________________________

Smaller Version

Read a chapter book.
Summarize each chapter. Cut out the pages.
Staple on the left side to make a mini-book.

Chapter # ____ Summary	Chapter # ____ Summary
______________________	______________________
______________________	______________________
______________________	______________________
______________________	______________________
______________________	______________________
Chapter # ____ Summary	**Chapter # ____ Summary**
______________________	______________________
______________________	______________________
______________________	______________________
______________________	______________________
______________________	______________________
Chapter # ____ Summary	**Chapter # ____ Summary**
______________________	______________________
______________________	______________________
______________________	______________________
______________________	______________________
______________________	______________________

Interacting with Text

Introduction

Research shows that when students make personal connections with text, they are more likely to enjoy that text. This positive experience creates lifelong readers. Giving students opportunities to analyze, critique, judge, and respond to text helps them create emotional connections to the stories. The following activities encourage students to explore concepts presented in a text and also what they bring to that text.

Road Trip!

Ask students if they have ever taken a family trip in a car. Have a few volunteers share their experiences. Then, introduce a story about travel, such as *Tulip Sees America* by Cynthia Rylant (Scholastic, 2002), a story about a man who takes his dog on a trip across the United States. Ask, "Which state do you think was the man's favorite? Why?" After hearing a few responses, give each student a copy of the Road Trip! reproducible (page 74). Let each student think of her favorite place to travel by car. Explain that the place could be very far away or just down the street. Have each student write about her favorite car trip on the reproducible. She may also draw a picture of herself in the driver's seat (or in the rear passenger's seat since she is more likely to sit there). Create a display by taping the reproducibles around a map titled "We're Going on a Road Trip!"

Advice Column

Explain that an *advice column* is an item in a newspaper that gives suggestions to people who want help solving their problems. Read the book *Weslandia* by Paul Fleischman (Candlewick Press, 2002). Ask, "Did Wesley have trouble making friends at the beginning of the story? Did he have friends at the end of the book? What happened to help Wesley make friends with his classmates?" Ask if there could have been another way for Wesley to make friends. Direct students to write advice columns to Wesley. Give each student one strip of white construction paper approximately 3" x 12" (8 cm x 30 cm). Have students advise Wesley about good ways to make friends. Have students start their columns with the greeting *Dear Wesley*. Other books whose characters will work with this activity are *The Grouchy Ladybug* by Eric Carle (HarperCollins, 1986), *Chester's Way* by Kevin Henkes (Greenwillow Books, 1991), *The Rainbow Fish* by Marcus Pfister (North-South Books, 1992), and *Swimmy* by Leo Lionni (Knopf, 1973). When students finish, display the columns on a bulletin board covered with newsprint.

Name ______________________

Road Trip!

Write about your favorite car trip on the lines below. Draw yourself in the car and color it.

____

____

____

____

____

____

Interacting with Opinions

Interacting with text involves sharing personal opinions. This activity provides an example of how points of view create reactions to text. Have each student cut out a large egg shape from white construction paper. The eggs need to be large enough to accommodate a few sentences in student handwriting. Read *An Extraordinary Egg* by Leo Lionni (Bantam Doubleday Dell, 1998). One of the characters in this book, Jessica, makes a decision to bring home a mysterious egg. As you read the story aloud, have students think about whether that was a good decision. After sharing the book, ask, "Do you think it was a good decision for Jessica to bring home the egg? Why or why not? Give examples from the book to support your answer." Have students write their responses on the paper eggs. Emphasize that there is no wrong answer since you are asking for their opinions. Assign students to small groups and have them share their responses. Cut a large nest from a piece of brown paper. Staple the nest onto a bulletin board and staple the eggs on top of the nest. Add the title "Our Egg-cellent Opinions."

Learning Lessons from Literature

Introduce *Strega Nona* by Tomie dePaola (Simon & Schuster, 1979) by explaining that one of the characters, Big Anthony, makes a mistake. Tell students that you want them to decide if Big Anthony learns from his mistake. Read (or have students read) *Strega Nona*. Ask, "What was Big Anthony's mistake?" (He made pasta in Strega Nona's magic pot without permission. The pasta overtook the town.) Ask, "Do you think Big Anthony learned his lesson? Why or why not?" Have students write their responses on the Anthony's Lesson reproducible (page 76). Assign students to pairs. Encourage them to share their responses with their partners. As an extra treat, provide construction paper and have students draw the spaghetti taking over the town. Allow students to stick cooked, cooled pasta to their drawings.

Friendship Connections

Use literature to explore friendship. Ask, "What do you look for in a friend?" Allow a few students to share their ideas. Read a book about friendship, such as *Horrible Harry in Room 2B* by Suzy Kline (Puffin, 1997). Have students think about whether they would like to have a friend like Harry. Give each student a piece of paper and a pencil. Tell students to write letters to Harry. Direct students to start the letters with the greeting *Dear Harry*. Have them state whether they would like Harry as a friend. Tell students to use examples from the book to support their positions. Have students sign the letters when they finish.

Name ______________________

Anthony's Lesson

Do you think Big Anthony learned his lesson? Why or why not?

Prescription for Student Solutions

Have students pose as doctors for a day. Ask, "What does a doctor do if a patient does not feel well?" Discuss how the doctor figures out what is wrong and how she may give instructions about what to do to get well or prescribe some medicine. Read A *Bad Case of Stripes* by David Shannon (Scholastic, 1998). In the story, Camilla does not feel well. Read up to page 23 in the book, when a woman tries to cure Camilla and causes Camilla to become part of her own bedroom. (Her mouth becomes her bed, her nose is the dresser, etc.) Ask, "What would you do to help Camilla get better?" Give each student a copy of the Prescription for Stripes reproducible (page 78). Have each student write a prescription that gives Camilla advice about what will make her feel better. Have students write their responses on the reproducibles. When they finish, ask, "What did you recommend?" Have a few students share their solutions. Say, "Let's see what happens in the story." Continue reading the book. After reading the story, ask, "Do you think your prescription would have worked?" Below the prescriptions on the reproducibles, have students draw pictures of how Camilla feels after taking their prescriptions.

Creating Story Sequels

Select a book and show students an illustration that depicts the main character. Ask, "Who do you think this person is? Why do you think so?" Confirm with students that the character is the main character in the story. Tell students the setting of the story and give them some background information about that setting. After reading the story, ask specific questions related to the story and have students suggest possible sequels that can be written for this story. Have them think of what happens next. Ask, "Where do the main characters go? What happens to them? What adventures do they have?" Have each student select a book to read and instruct him to write a sequel for it. (Some students may need to draw pictures and dictate text.) When the sequels are complete, have each student share his story with a partner. Let students add construction-paper covers. Store the sequels in the class library next to their matching original stories. Encourage students who read the original stories to read the sequels, as well.

Moral Lessons

Select a collection of fables, such as Arnold Lobel's *Fables* (HarperCollins, 1983). Two present-day versions of Aesop's fables that are appropriate for this activity are *The Tortoise and the Hare* adapted and illustrated by Janet Stevens (Holiday House, 1985) and *The Ant and the Grasshopper* retold and illustrated by Amy Lowry Poole (Holiday House, 2000). Explain that a *fable* is a short story that has a moral, or lesson, that can often be applied to a real-life situation. Read a few of the fables aloud for examples. Instruct students to think of times when they learned lessons. Have each student write a story that includes a moral at the end. Collect the student fables into a class book. Read one fable each day and let volunteers talk about how the lesson taught in the fable applies to their lives.

Prescription for Stripes

Write a prescription to help Camilla feel better. When your teacher finishes reading the book, draw a picture of Camilla under the prescription.

Patient Name Camilla Date ______________

Doctor (your name) ______________________

Here is what Camilla should do to feel better: ______________

____

____

____

Rx

Signature ______________________

Forming Opinions

Select a book that contains a main character whose decisions have a direct influence on the outcome of the story. Some examples are favorite fairy tales, such as *Jack and the Bean Stalk* and *Little Red Riding Hood.* Two other possible books for this activity are *The Rainbow Fish* by Marcus Pfister (North-South Books, 1992) and *The Story of Jumping Mouse* by John Steptoe (HarperCollins, 1984). Prior to reading the story, describe one of the decisions of the main character. Ask students to think about whether that decision is good or bad while they listen to the story. For example, in *The Story of Jumping Mouse*, Jumping Mouse decides to give several things away. After reading the book aloud, ask "Do you think it was a good decision for Jumping Mouse to give away his powers?" Have students discuss the topic in small groups. Remind students there are no wrong answers; they are just stating their own opinions and backing them up.

Connecting Text with Various Generations

Use a book about an older relative to help students understand people from a different generation. For example, read *Grandfather's Journey* by Allen Say (Houghton Mifflin, 1993). Ask, "What do you think the author meant when he wrote *I think I know my grandfather now?*" Next, give each student a piece of paper, a drinking straw, and a half-sheet of construction paper. Direct each student to fold the whole sheet of paper in half vertically, turn the paper so that the fold is the bottom edge, and write her response to the question on the paper. Direct her to place the straw vertically in the middle of the folded paper. Have each student glue the straw to the paper. Then, have her draw a large triangle on the half-sheet of construction paper, cut it out, and glue (or tape) the triangular sail to the straw to make the paper look like a sailboat. While the glue dries, have students share their responses with partners. Create a display titled "Sailing through Grandfather's Journey" by stapling the boats to a bulletin board. Make sure students' responses are facing out.

Independent Reading Log

Use the Independent Reading Log reproducible (page 80) to keep track of reading homework or as a log for independent reading in the classroom. If students use the log in class, consider using the information as an informal assessment tool. Students will use the reproducible to rate books they read. Have each student read a book independently. Then, have her write the title and author of the book on the reading log. On the next line, which says "Book Summary," direct each student to write one or two sentences explaining what the book is about. Remind students that a summary does not include the details of the book, just the main idea. Then, have each student rate the book on a scale of one to five. Students will color in the book shapes to rate books. Explain that coloring in one book means a student did not like the book very much while coloring all five books means she loved the book. Coloring in three books means it was "just OK." Finally, direct students to explain their ratings. Why was it great, or why was it terrible? Encourage students to keep track of the books they read independently by using the log.

Name ______________________________

Independent Reading Log

After reading a book, write the information on the lines.

Book Title ______________________________

Author's Name ______________________________

Book Summary ______________________________

____

____

Rate the book.

Why did you give the book that rating?

____

Book Title ______________________________

Author's Name ______________________________

Book Summary ______________________________

____

____

Rate the book.

Why did you give the book that rating?

____